Getting the Most Out of

Morning Message

and Other Shared Writing

Lessons

Great techniques

for teaching beginning writers

by writi...

Name charts
p. 31

Wordless stories
p. 105

Old Woman
who swallowed
a Fly

by Carleer

and Mary Br

SCHOLASTIC
PROFESSIONAL BOOKS

NEW YORK • TORONTO • LONDON • AUCKLAND • SYDNEY
MEXICO CITY • NEW DELHI • HONG KONG

Dedication

To my principal and friend, Joanne Ibbotson,
for your belief in me right from the start.

To my mother, Mary Aguiar daCruz, for the blessed woman you were,
and my father, Edward, for teaching me to reach for the stars.

To my son, Stephen, and my daughter, Lesley,
for making my life so much richer.

To my remarkable husband, Dick, for being the anchor in my life.

cdp

For Jay, my dearest friend, who makes so many
of life's moments precious.

mbs

Front cover design by Kathy Massaro
Cover photograph by Jay M. Schulman
Interior design by Kathy Massaro

ISBN 0-590-36516-9

Contents

In Appreciation

I am fortunate to be in the company of *extraordinary* students, parents, and teaching professionals who contribute to my literacy. This book is a tribute to their support and help. I acknowledge with special gratitude:

Joan Clemmons, DonnaLynn Cooper, and Lois Laase, classroom teachers, and Mary Dill, principal at Rolling Valley Elementary School in Fairfax County, Virginia, for beginning the journey into language arts instruction with me.

Keith Hall and Phyllis McKoy, assistant principals, and my colleagues and friends at Centre Ridge Elementary School in Fairfax County, Virginia, for the privilege of working and learning beside you these past eight years. You exemplify the *best* of the teaching profession.

The diverse and wonderful students of Centre Ridge Elementary School who teach me daily what is important in reading and writing. —*cdp*

I believe you never write a book like this alone. Within its pages are the lives and experiences that have touched my life both professionally and personally. I am grateful for the opportunity to work with Janet Funk, the principal at William Halley Elementary. Your leadership is matchless as is your strong belief that all students can learn.

I thank my colleagues, the students and parents at William Halley Elementary where I've learned much in the three years since the school opened its doors to children. To my dear friend and fellow practitioner, Terry Creamer, I thank you for the never ending invitations to come into your classroom and for sharing your expertise throughout the writing of this book.

Thank you to my mom, Margaret Browning, for her belief in me always.

My deepest appreciation to my nine siblings and their families, who have always been there for me and continue to be there. A special thanks to my brother Charles Browning for reading and responding to the drafts along the way.

To Jay, my partner in life, thank you with heartfelt love and gratitude for your unwavering inspiration and confidence. —*mbs*

A special thanks to Centre Ridge Elementary School teachers, William Halley teachers, and other colleagues who shared ideas and their classrooms for this book: Katie Abruzzino, Gina Bangert, Linda Bowlin, Carrie Campbell, Sarah Cobb, Suzanne Comer, Molly Connolly, Terry Creamer, Patty Cruzan, Amy Dux, Jacqueline Fee, Laura Kurner, Amy Linder, Pamela Mahoney, Sally Murray, Joe Silva, Helene Stapleton, and Cathy Yerington.

We thank Terry Cooper and Wendy Murray, editors at Scholastic, for inviting us to tell our teacher stories.

Lastly, we are appreciative of the opportunity to learn from each other, and for the special journey we have experienced as *shared writers*.

cdp ✿ *mbs*

Introduction

Poet and writer Georgia Heard says "Memory's cloak is usually an image…." I have a disparaging image of myself as a young writer that I still carry with me today. When I entered kindergarten, I spoke only Portuguese. Writing was difficult throughout my school years. I had no writing models to follow and struggled to find the correct words to use when I wrote. Writing—symbolized by the teacher's red pen—was a dreaded experience and something I thought I wasn't very good at doing. It wasn't until much later as a young teacher, when I studied the work of Donald Graves, that I learned about the process of writing and the importance of teacher demonstrations. I realized the power of modeling the writing process for my students and was determined to show them how to become writers through shared writing experiences. Consequently, I became a teacher of writers, and a writer myself.

—Carleen daCruz Payne

Carleen's words may mirror some of the painful experiences with writing that many of us have encountered in school and that frequently influence us throughout our lives. Our decision to write this book is a result of many conversations—at meetings, conferences, or just over dinner—about how teachers can profoundly influence the perceptions young children have of themselves as writers. Writing is not easy. It is full of challenges for young children. They must learn much about how written language works—much of what is so automatic for us.

In this book, we describe ways that teachers can write *with* children to support and extend their understanding about writing and to help them cross the bridge to independent writing. We step inside kindergarten, first, and second grade classrooms at the William Halley and Centre Ridge Elementary schools to catch a glimpse of what happens when the teachers and students share in the writing together. We look at how shared writing changes over time—from the time the teacher is the primary scribe to the time students share the pen to write. We examine what students learn from shared writing. We consider how shared writing helps students to learn concepts about print, a sense of audience and purpose, forms of writing, and the ways words work, and to extend their understanding of literature. We offer ideas and suggestions to teachers who are trying to incorporate more shared writing into their schedules and across the curriculum. We also propose ways teachers can reach out to parents to gain their support in reinforcing and extending their schools' writing programs by writing at home with their children.

Finally, we've included an appendix that contains publisher information, professional resources, the children's literature selections mentioned throughout the book, selected references, computer software, and assessment forms.

If you're a teacher of young writers, we hope this book will provide you with some helpful ideas for writing with students, help you sort out or extend some of what you've tried, or simply reinforce some of your current teaching practices.

In the words of what was once Carleen's first language we express our belief that—*o direito de aprender a lêr e a escrever pertence a toudos estudantes*—the right to read and write belongs to every student.

cdp   mbs

CHAPTER 1

Shared Writing

"Learners need demonstrations of how writing works."

—New Zealand Ministry of Education, Dancing With a Pen

Help me out, what should I write next? Is that the same or different? Where should I write that? You're right, stove *begins like* stop.

Carrie Campbell and her first graders are gathered around a large sheet of seamless paper, deep in the midst of talking and writing about how two versions of the familiar tale of *The Three Little Pigs* are alike and different. During the past week, Carrie has read aloud numerous versions of the story to the students. They've discussed the story lines, compared the books, and made personal connections. Now huddled together on the floor, marker pen in hand, Carrie demonstrates how writers organize and record ideas and thoughts on paper in different ways. She writes in front of the students as they talk about what, how, and where to write their ideas on a comparison chart like the Venn diagram in the photograph. By writing with her first graders, Carrie helps her students learn to write and write to learn.

Above: Carrie Campbell and her first grade students compare two versions of The Three Little Pigs *in a shared writing lesson.*

What is shared writing?

Shared writing is writing *with* students. It is a way of introducing students to writing *through* writing. When teachers write with students, they can make visible what is often invisible. By seeing and hearing an experienced writer write, students begin to understand the connections between oral language and written language. They observe concepts about print in action. They realize that writers can record ideas in a variety of ways and forms; they recognize that writing serves different purposes. Shared writing can serve as a tool for helping students accomplish an activity they can't yet do on their own; it can bridge the way to independent writing.

What does shared writing look like?

There's no one way to do shared writing. At William Halley Elementary and Centre Ridge Elementary schools, where we serve as reading/language arts resource teachers, shared writing is used for many different purposes and in a wide variety of ways. When the teachers in our schools make decisions about how to plan a shared writing lesson for students, they consider the following:

- purpose for writing
- skills to be developed (based on assessments of what students already know and can do)
- level of teacher support or guidance needed for the writing task
- number of students (whole class, small group, individual)
- who will do the writing (teacher, teacher and students)

Shared writing lessons may take almost any form—recounting shared experiences, innovations on stories, making lists, writing procedures, letters, observations, messages, newsletters, and more. During shared writing, the teacher and students talk and decide what they want to write together. There may be an intended focus, but the content and construction of the message often unfolds as they talk. As the ideas are negotiated and decided upon, the teacher may act as the primary scribe or invite the students to share the pen.

The length of each shared writing session is flexible. The lesson may last anywhere from five to 20 minutes; it might be completed in one day or continue over several. For example, Gina Bangert spends ten minutes of her kindergarten class' circle time every day writing the daily news with her students. When the class hatched eggs during a farm unit, she and her students spent time each day for two weeks recording their continuing observations in a class learning log.

Many teachers organize an open area in the classroom around an easel, chalkboard, or computer to make it easy to write with their students. Laura Kurner's first graders sometimes gather around the easel with her to write the class news on newsprint. Other times, they pull their chairs up to the computer and compose there. Molly Connolly likes her second graders to move their chairs around the overhead projector so it's easy for them to see and contribute when they write the class message together. When Terry Creamer meets with a small group of her first graders to write, they gather around a kidney-shaped table, making it easy for everyone to add something to the writing. To better illustrate the range of what shared writing can look like, let's step inside a few classrooms at Halley and Centre Ridge schools.

After a visit from Firefighter Bill, who brought his equipment to school and talked about fire safety in the home, Sarah Cobb's kindergarten class met in the open area on the rug to write a thank-you note. Sarah and the kindergartners discussed what they might write in the note, the format they'd use, and where they'd begin writing. Then, together they went on to compose the message word by word. While they were writing, Sarah and the students reread the message up to each new word they added. They stopped to talk about the sounds they heard in the words they wanted to write, why it was important to leave spaces to make it easy for Firefighter Bill to read, and how to end the note. While Sarah acted as the scribe, she and the students turned their ideas into written language.

Laura Kurner posts the news she and the first graders write on their classroom door.

Early in the school year, during center time or at the beginning of writing workshop, first grade teacher Terry Creamer meets with small groups of three to five students who are struggling with writing independently in their journals. Terry knows that these students need a high level of support and encouragement in order to get their ideas down on paper. She helps them decide what topic to write about. She guides them as they learn how to say words slowly so they can analyze the sounds they hear and predict what letters they'll need to write. She shows them how to reread their writing to figure out what word comes next. She frequently refers to things she's focused on in the morning messages the class writes together each day (see Chapter 3, p.39).

Terry supports her first graders' attempts throughout the writing; she questions to get them to use what they already know, demonstrates to show them what she means, and shares the pencil to fill in the parts that they can't yet do on their own. Even those students who can read and write very little can participate in the writing process when they share the writing with Terry.

A small group of first graders write in their journals with help from teacher Terry Creamer. The students are the apprentices, working beside the more experienced writer. ▶

Why use shared writing?

Shared writing provides a basis for thinking, talking, writing, reading and listening. Writing texts with students helps them explore language and build an understanding of how it functions. It provides them with opportunities to learn how to construct and organize ideas for particular purposes. Demonstrations of both writing and writing behaviors show students what writers do—the process they themselves will use when they write independently.

Although shared writing is only one of the components of a balanced reading and writing program (see Chapter 2, page 21), it powerfully supports students' understanding of written language. It helps students realize that writing is a process used to share ideas and communicate meaning. When teachers write with students, they demonstrate that:

❈ **Writers communicate ideas and thoughts on paper.**

We'll be having a visitor today. Officer Yates will be talking to us about safety. We might want to include something about that in our morning message today.

After first grade students wrote the morning message with their teacher, she had students find a word in the message and circle it. ▶

❈ **Thought processes occur as you write.**

Oh, I need to remember to leave a space before I write the next word, so it's easy to read.

Terry Creamer helps first grader Karan remember to leave a space between words as he helps write the morning message. ▶

❊ **Talking about experiences can elicit ideas.**
What did you think about the story that Jamil's grandmother chose to read to the class yesterday?

❊ **Writing can communicate ideas.**
Maybe today we can write to Jamil's grandmother to thank her for coming in to read to us yesterday. We might want to write some of the ideas we've talked about. Jamil, what would you like me to write in the letter to your Grandma?

❊ **Writers use different ways to plan what to write (such as brainstorming, drawing, and graphic organizers).**
Now, let's reread the informational web on zoo animals that we wrote together yesterday and today.

Before Amy Dux's first grade class visited the zoo, they prepared by writing an informational web about zoo animals. ▶

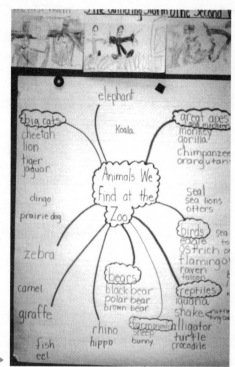

❊ **Writers draft ideas (ways to start and end, expand ideas, and use interesting language).**
Now that we've brainstormed some of the story language the author William Steig used in his story about Sylvester, let's see if we can include some of his language to write a retelling of the story.

Second graders in Molly Connolly's class include some of the literary language in the retelling of Sylvester and the Magic Pebble. ▶

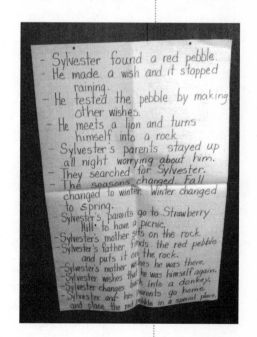

❊ **Writers use strategies such as rereading to check, confirm, or add to the writing.**
Follow along while I reread to check to see if we've already told that part.

❊ **Writing can be changed and refined.**
Lucas noticed that we left out the part about our picnic lunch at the zoo. Show us where we could write that part, if we decide to add it.

❊ **Sequence is important.**
What will we tell people to do first if they want to know how to make applesauce? What would be the next step?

✤ **Writers need to understand concepts about print (such as direction of print, one-to-one correspondence, return sweep, concept of letter and word).**

Who can show me where I begin writing? What word do I write first? I've come to the end of this line, where do I go now?

A first grade student shows Carleen where she should begin the next word in the message. ▶

✤ **Conventions of written language are tools writers need (such as punctuation, capitalization, grammar).**

We forgot to use a question mark someplace in our morning message. Who can find where we need to put it? How do you know it goes there?

✤ **Strategies help determine correct spelling.**

• Students learn how to say words slowly to listen for different letters, letter combinations, and sounds.

What letter sounds can you hear in went? *Say it slowly. (Child articulates the word slowly, but not isolating individual letter sounds.) What do you hear first? Say* went *again slowly. What do you hear next? What else do you hear?*

• Students learn how words work and how they look in the English language (letter patterns, how words are the same/different, how prefixes and suffixes are added).

What do you notice about the word today *in our message? That's right, two little words make a bigger word or a new word. Who knows what we call words like this?*

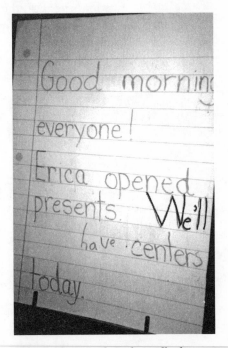

The students and teacher talk about how words work before, during, and after writing the morning message.

Say-It-Slowly Technique

Try this technique to teach students how to say words slowly and listen for the letter sounds they hear. You'll need: an elastic band (a cut-off pair of jockey briefs, for example), a large blank paper, and a marker. Tell the students that you're going to teach them a new game called "Say It Slowly." Show them the elastic band and demonstrate how the game works by slowly articulating a word while stretching the band. Be careful not to isolate individual letters. Have students pretend to stretch their own imaginary band and say the same word slowly with you. Continue with a few more words, each time stretching the band as you and the students say the word slowly. Now, ask the students to repeat one of the words they've already practiced, but this time, have them listen for the sounds they can hear in the word. Ask:

- *What letter sounds can you hear in...?*
- *What did you hear first?*
- *What did you hear next?*
- *What else did you hear?*

As students respond, use the marker to write the letter sounds students hear on the blank paper. Have the students repeat the word slowly, listening for other sounds, until they think they've heard all the sounds in the word. Accept the sounds they hear in any order. As the students learn how to hear sounds in words, use the above questions to help them to think about the sequence of the sounds they hear in words. Encourage students to use this technique during shared writing and independent writing times.

A kindergartner in Amy Linder's class, who is writing in his journal during independent writing, says a word slowly to listen for the sounds he hears. ▶

❄ **Genres and forms used in writing can vary.**

Since we've been reading riddle books, some of you have said you'd like to try writing a riddle. What might we write a riddle about?

❄ **Designs and layouts of text can vary.**

We have all the ideas for our own big book version of The Gingerbread Man, *so let's think about how we want it to look.*

❄ **Writing can be read by others.**

Let's read our story together. Jenna, come up and point while we read. Before we read, show us where we begin. Then, which way do we go? And where do we go when we get to the end of the line? Everybody else follow along as Jenna points.

The students read along in Sally Murray's class as a kindergartner points.

❄ **Writing informs others.**

Mrs. Schulman wrote us a note to thank us for letting her take our pictures for the book she's writing. Let's put it in the message center, so you can read it again.

Quick Tip

Use shared writing texts produced by students as part of the core of reading material. Texts created from students' own experiences, using familiar language patterns, make good beginning reading material.

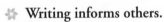

Making the most of shared writing

At Halley and Centre Ridge, we and the teachers we work alongside strongly believe that assessment informs teaching. Our kindergarten, first, and second grade teachers plan shared writing demonstrations relevant to the students' levels and current needs. The shared writing activities are based on ongoing assessment information and the learning goals we've identified.

Our teachers constantly observe students and use a variety of techniques and record keeping instruments to collect information, to find out what our budding writers already know and can do, and what they need to learn. Teachers gather information through observation, work samples, and student and parent conferences. The assessment is embedded in the day-to-day teaching and learning. It allows the teacher to establish a baseline for charting students' literacy growth. It also allows the teachers to consider and reflect on their own teaching decisions and approaches.

During the first month of school, the teachers use the following assessment tools to begin building a profile of each student:

Alphabet Recognition Record Sheet

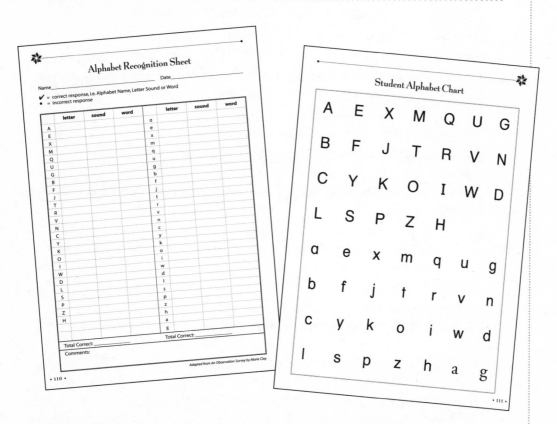

In kindergarten and grade one, teachers assess students' knowledge of the alphabet letter names and letter sounds (Clay, 1991). It helps to know which students need additional help in learning the alphabet.

Alphabet Recognition Record Sheet

Name: Miguel   Date: 9/12/97

✓ = correct response, i.e. Alphabet Name, Letter Sound or Word
• = incorrect response

	letter	sound	word		letter	sound	word
A	✓		apple	a	✓		
E	✓			e	•		
X	✓			x	✓		
M	✓		miguel	m	✓		
Q	•			q	•		
U	•			u	•		
G	✓			g	•		
B	✓			b	✓		
F	✓			f	•		
J	✓			j	✓		
T	✓			t	•		
R	✓			r	✓		
V	•			v	•		
N	✓			n	✓		
C	✓			c	•		
Y				y	•		
K	✓			k	✓		
O	✓			o	✓		
I	✓			i	✓		
W	•			w	•		
D	✓			d	•		
L				l	✓		
S	✓			s	✓		
P				p	b/no-b?		
Z	✓			z	✓		
H	✓			h	•		
				a	•		
				g	•		

Total Correct: 21   Total Correct: 13

Comments: Said "M" was what his name starts with; Unknown uppercase: Q, U, V, Y, W Unknown lowercase: e, q,u, g, f, t, v, c, y, w, d, h, a, g; went through uppercase letters quickly; much slower with the lowercase letters

Adapted from An Observation Survey by Marie Clay

Miguel's completed Alphabet Recognition Record Sheet

How to Use the Alphabet Recognition Record Sheet

1. Sit beside the student.
2. Give the child the Student Alphabet Chart (see Appendix).
3. Begin by asking the student: "What are these?"
4. Point to each letter across the line and ask: "What is this one?"
5. If the student does not answer, use one of the following questions:

   Do you know its name?
   What sound does it make?
   Do you know a word that begins like that?

6. Use the Alphabet Recognition Record Sheet to record responses (see Appendix).
7. Count as correct if the letter name, letter sound, or a word beginning with the letter was given.
8. Total the correct uppercase letters and lowercase letters identified and record in the comments section any observations during the completion of the task.

Observe/Analyze/Reflect

- What does the child call the letters? (A, B, C's, alphabet, words, numbers, etc.)
- Which way does the child identify a letter—alphabet name, sound or word?
- Which letter(s) does the child reverse or confuse?
- Which letters are known/unknown?

Student Writing Sample

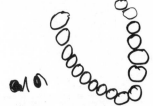

Writing Sample Assessment Record
For Early Writing

Name _Laura_   Date(s) _9/97_

To build a profile of the writer use a different colored highlighter pen to mark the learning behaviors observed each time a writing sample is reviewed. In the comments section make a note or two about future areas of focus.

Concepts/Conventions of Print
Knows where to begin writing
Knows writing moves left-to-right and top-to-bottom
Leaves spaces between words *beginning*
Correct letter formation *(except Y)*
Concept of letter
Concept of word
Uppercase and lowercase letters used conventionally
Approximate spelling
Conventional spelling of frequently used words
Uses punctuation: periods; question marks; exclamation marks; quotations; commas; apostrophes
Other: *9/97 was able to point to words as she read to me; mixes capitals and lowercase letters*

Understands That Writing Conveys a Message
Drawing/pictures
Scribble
Print-like symbols
Strings of letters
Writes own name: first name; last name
Letter/sound relationships: beginning; beginning/ending; beginning/medial/ending
Labels for pictures
Words
Phrases (groups of words)
Sentence
Several sentences
Beginning, middle and end
Details or vocabulary specific to topic
Central idea organized and elaborated
Other:

9/97
Comments: *I beginning to leave spaces; had difficulty reading because words are not well-spaced; wrote on own — no adult help*

Designed by Mary Browning Schulman and Carleen daCruz Payne

▲ I gave a necklace and clip-on
earrings for my Mom
— Laura
Grade 1

Writing Sample Assessment Record
For Early Writing

Name _Trevor_   Date(s) _9/97_

To build a profile of the writer use a different colored highlighter pen to mark the learning behaviors observed each time a writing sample is reviewed. In the comments section make a note or two about future areas of focus.

Concepts/Conventions of Print
Knows where to begin writing
Knows writing moves left-to-right and top-to-bottom
Leaves spaces between words *not enough evidence (9/97)*
Correct letter formation *except Y*
Concept of letter
Concept of word
Uppercase and lowercase letters used conventionally
Approximate spelling
Conventional spelling of frequently used words *I, AM, Tree, A, MY*
Uses punctuation: periods; question marks; exclamation marks; quotations; commas; apostrophes
Other: *9/97 numbers on writing are mine to help me remember how I pointed and read; mixed capitals and lowercase letters*

Understands That Writing Conveys a Message
Drawing/pictures
Scribble
Print-like symbols
Strings of letters
Writes own name: first name; last name
Letter/sound relationships: beginning; beginning/ending; beginning/medial/ending
Labels for pictures
Words
Phrases (groups of words) *L→R and T↓B*
Sentence *(but not written L→R and T↓B)*
Several sentences
Beginning, middle and end
Details or vocabulary specific to topic
Central idea organized and elaborated
Other:

9/97
Comments: *T. unaware of importance of convention of L→R; struggled to reread the message; we looked at what Bill Martin did when he wrote his text for Brown Bear.... for L→R & top-to-bottom directionality of print*

Designed by Mary Browning Schulman and Carleen daCruz Payne

I am with my
adopted tree
— Trevor
Kindergarten ▶

At the beginning of the school year, teachers ask students to create a writing sample by drawing a picture and/or writing about a topic of their choice. They encourage students to write about something or someone they know and care about. Students usually create the sample in one sitting without the help of the teacher. Teachers use an assessment tool such as the Writing Sample Assessment Record For Early Writing (see Appendix) to highlight the learning behaviors they observe as they analyze the student sample. Some teachers record with a different colored highlighter pen each time they review a new sample to build a picture of the student writer over time.

Observe/Analyze/Reflect

- How does the child write to convey a message?
- What does the child know about letters, words, phrases, sentences, stories?
- How does the child use space on the paper?
- What does the child understand about the directionality of print in writing?
- What does the child understand about written conventions of print such as punctuation, use of uppercase-lowercase letters, and how words work?

Writing Vocabulary

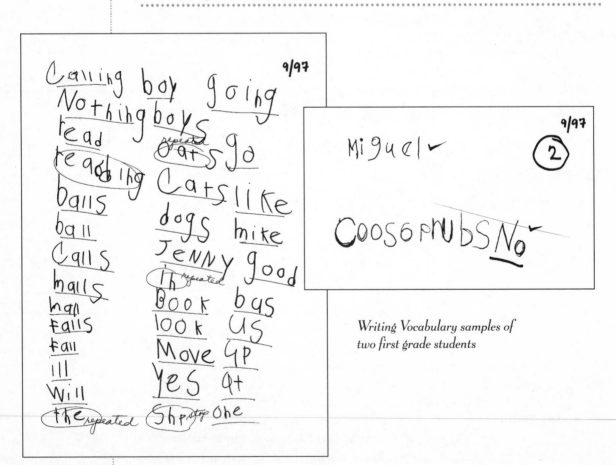

Writing Vocabulary samples of two first grade students

A teacher can do this assessment any place at any time to find out what words and parts of words the child controls. At the beginning of the year and periodically during the school year, Centre Ridge and Halley teachers use the writing vocabulary to assess all the words a student can write independently in ten minutes (Clay, 1991). The teacher gives the students a blank piece of paper and pencil and says: *I want to see how many words you can write. Can you write your name?* If necessary, the teacher can prompt the students by suggesting categories. For example: *Do you know how to write any... animal words? color words? number words? little words? things you eat? places you go? names of people in your family?*

Observe/Analyze/Reflect

- How many words does the child know how to write?
- What is the type of correctly spelled known words that the child can write?
- What does the child know about letters and letter formation?
- How does the child attend to space on the page, and between letters, words, and lines?
- Does the child write left to right and top to bottom?
- Are there confusions?
- Is the child able to link words? (can, man, Dan; went, want, won't)
- Does the child use analogies/associations? (up/down; in/to/into; yellow/sun)
- Does the child know how to use word endings? (jump, jumps, jumping, jumped)
- How does the child use uppercase/lowercase letters?

Writing Letters

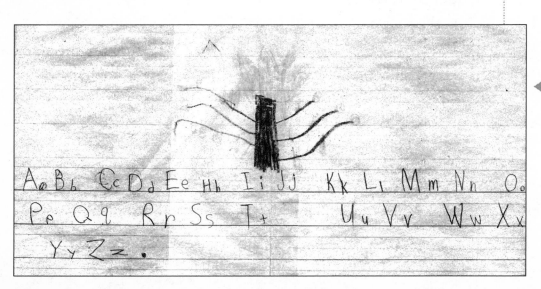

◀ *Here's how a first grader wrote the alphabet letters he knew in September.*

At the beginning of the year, in kindergarten and first grade, teachers ask their students to write all the letters of the alphabet that they know. They often do this in an open area or a hallway where there's no alphabet chart for students to copy. The teacher says: *I want you to write all the letters in the alphabet that you know how to write. Start with "A" and keep going. If you know how to write a letter more than one way, write it another way.*

Observe/Analyze/Reflect

- How many letters can the child write?
- Which letters can the child write? (letters in name; uppercase only; uppercase and lowercase)
- How does the child use space on the paper, between letters, at the end of a line?
- Does the writing go left to right and top to bottom?
- Are the letters in sequence?
- Are there any confusions in sequence? If so, where is the confusion? (near beginning, middle, end)
- Are there any reversals?
- How does the child form the letters? (If you have a question about any particular letter, ask the child to write the letter while you observe.)

Along with these assessment measures, teachers at Centre Ridge and Halley take special note of students' involvement, understanding, and insights during:

- shared writing
- independent writing
- read aloud time
- shared reading
- guided reading
- DEAR (Drop Everything And Read) time
- oral discussions

The teachers record anecdotal notes, use running records to observe and analyze students' reading behaviors, and confer with students to gain information about their thinking about reading, writing, and learning.

It's the assessment information that will answer the question: *What do I teach?* And, it's the assessment information that will help you plan and focus your instruction to get the most out of shared writing lessons with your students. As you assess what your students can already do as writers, think about how to build on what they know. Consider every opportunity to write as a chance to demonstrate something about writing.

CHAPTER 2

A Classroom Environment for Shared Writing

"Granted, there are some systematic and highly structured elements to teaching writing, but I didn't realize until I wrote the introduction to Nancie Atwell's In the Middle that good writing doesn't result from any particular methodology. Rather, the remarkable work of her students was a result of the conditions for learning she created in her classroom."

—Donald Graves,
A Fresh Look At Writing

At Centre Ridge and Halley, when we establish our classrooms for literacy, we try to provide the same opportunities for writing that we have for speaking, listening, and reading. We collaborate with students and help them see writing as a purposeful activity. We make every effort to provide an atmosphere conducive to risk-taking. To allow for shared writing, we think about classrooms with the following key points in mind.

Above: Carleen daCruz Payne visits a first grade classroom for some shared writing.

A Balanced Literacy Program

We are asked frequently how young students become readers and writers. We've found that there's no magical ingredient that gets students to read or write, but we know we can provide good first teaching through a balanced literacy program. Let's use Halley and Centre Ridge classrooms to view a balanced literacy program.

1

2

Writing To/For

Amy Dux writes to her students, demonstrating that writing serves a purpose. You can find opportunities to write to your students daily: recording the class schedule, creating the morning message or daily news, or writing about procedures in the classroom.

Reading To

Terry Creamer demonstrates the importance of reading by reading aloud to a group of first grade students. It's a great idea to read to students daily. You can select a variety of forms, genres, styles of writing, and topics of interest, knowing that you're building background knowledge for story structure and the language of books.

3

Reading With Students

Carleen daCruz Payne selects and reads big books, small books, and charts for shared reading. During the reading, she may point to the words or locate special words. Carleen and the students revisit, reread, and talk about the texts often.

Sometimes Terry Creamer does guided reading with one student or a small group. She selects texts to match the abilities of her readers. During guided reading, her students practice the reading skills and strategies they've learned, while Terry observes how effectively they use them.

Writing *With* Students ▶

Writing with students is shared writing. Suzanne Comer writes ideas or messages as she talks and guides her first graders through the process of composing. As students compose with her, she asks questions to clarify the meaning of the message, talks about its purpose and intended audience, and invites students to share the pen and write the parts they can.

▲ Reading *By* Students

We try to provide time for students to read and reread familiar texts on their own. If you haven't already established a DEAR (Drop Everything And Read) time, you might want to try it. Students in Terry Creamer's first grade classroom create book baskets of familiar reading and use written material on display—such as charts, poems, messages, songs, and student-written stories—to "read the room."

▲ Writing *By* Students

Students in Amy Linder's class write independently four to five times a week. Amy establishes a predictable structure and routine. She gives students choices about what to write, responds through conferences and sharing circles, and provides direct instruction through focus lessons. She encourages students to experiment with a range of genres and forms across the curriculum.

We've seen that when our students have a balanced literacy program—reading and writing to, with, and by—they understand what reading and writing are for as well as how to do them.

Classroom Space

In the beginning of the school year, the classroom is "under construction," and the "bare bones" look can be surprising. In his book *Life in a Crowded Place*, Ralph Peterson talks about building community in the classroom. He says, "The primary goal at the beginning of a new year or term is to lead students to come together, form a group, and be there for one another."

Tip Box

What to Include In a Shared Writing Center

Conduct shared writing activities in a area where the whole class can be seated. Include an easel, chalkboard, pointer, and, if possible, a computer. Provide lots of writing materials and organize them in inexpensive containers for quick accessibility. Here are materials to consider:

- assorted markers, crayons, and colored pencils
- variety of paper: newsprint, chart, tag board, and construction
- staplers and staples
- pencils and erasers
- regular scissors and scissors with fancy cutting edges
- transparent tape and masking tape in assorted widths
- white glue and washable glitter glue
- white correction tape
- hole punch
- assorted magnets
- rulers and yardsticks
- binding machine and assorted sizes of plastic bindings
- yarn, string, and metal rings
- magnetic letters with magnetic boards
- wikki stix™ (waxy yarn)
- reference materials such as dictionaries and thesauri
- computer paper, diskettes, and software programs

Teachers at Centre Ridge and Halley welcome and value students' comments and thoughts. We know that our students will care more about learning in a classroom they've helped organize. So, with our students, we decide where to locate some of the meeting, work, and center areas. We talk about how to organize our library corner and how we want to use our bulletin board space. We make plans to adapt the room arrangement as our classroom activities change. By involving students in these decisions, we create a sense of togetherness and ownership in our learning community.

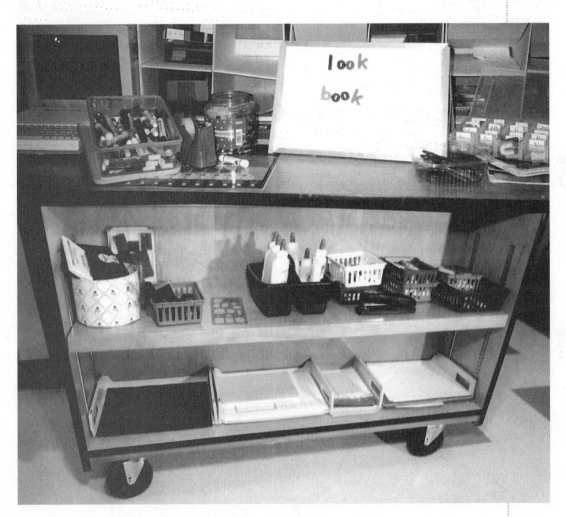

Amy Dux and her first graders use shared writing materials in a small space.

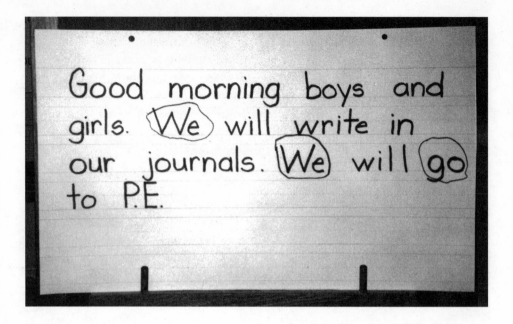

Schedule

Centre Ridge and Halley teachers work to establish daily, predictable schedules for their students. These include shared writing experiences for three to five days a week, keeping the number of sessions flexible depending on the activity and its purpose.

In kindergarten and first grade classrooms, we allot more time for shared writing, because students need many demonstrations on how written language works. In second grade classrooms, we engage students in more independent writing activities, so instruction is guided by individual and group needs.

The teachers experiment with different time frames and schedules. In Cathy Yerington's first grade classroom, shared writing—composing the morning message or rewriting a favorite poem or story—is often the first activity of the day. Sometimes she includes shared writing during science, social studies, or math times, when she and her first graders are working on a collaborative project. Activities such as recording scientific observations of seeds in a class learning log or creating an informational web for a social studies zoo unit provide Cathy's class with other shared writing opportunities. Notice how Cathy's daily class schedule integrates writing activities throughout the day.

Daily Schedule — Cathy Yerington's First Grade

9:00 – 9:30   **Circle Time**
Calendar; Weather; Shared Reading: Big Book/Small Book; Shared Writing: Morning Message/Daily News or Retelling of a Shared Experience or Innovation on a Text

9:30 – 9:50   **DEAR (Drop Everything & Read)**
First graders read independently. Cathy roves and meets with individual students on an as-need basis.

9:50 – 10:30   **Reading Workshop**
Cathy reads with small groups for guided reading while other students work at literacy centers.

10:30 – 11:15   **Writing Workshop**
Students write independently while Cathy provides individual or group support. Students share their writing.

11:15 – 12:00   **Lunch & Recess**

12:00 – 12:15   **Read Aloud**

12:15 – 1:15   **Math**

1:15 – 1:45   **Music/P.E.**

1:45 – 2:00   **Snack**

2:00 – 3:00   **Science/Social Studies**
Hands-on learning in the Content Areas; Some Shared Writing/Reading

3:00 – 3:30   **Closing/Dismissal**

Joe Silva, a second grade teacher, includes shared writing at the beginning of his class' writing workshop period. He says, "This gives me an opportunity to revisit an aspect of writing that I've already taught or to teach a new skill my students might use in their writing later. Starting this way also helps students settle into a writing frame of mind quickly when they're writing independently."

Daily Schedule - Joe Silva's Second Grade

9:00 – 9:15 **Class News**
Attendance; Calendar; Schedule; Message Board

9:15 – 10:15 **Writing Workshop**
Focus lesson on writing/shared writing. (15/20 min.)
Students write independently while Joe confers with individuals or small groups. (30 min.)
Students share writing. (10 min.)

10:15 – 11:15 **Reading Workshop**
DEAR Time: Students read independently while Joe reads individually with students at risk. (20 min.)
Guided Reading Groups with Joe; Students at Literacy Centers. (40 min.)

11:15 – 11:30 **Read Aloud**

11:30 – 12:00 **Music/P.E.**

12:00 – 12:45 **Lunch & Recess**

12:45 – 1:45 **Math**

1:45 – 2:45 **Science/Social Studies**
Content learning with Shared Reading/Writing activities as appropriate.

2:45 – 3:00 **Library Browsing**
Students browse through classroom library/visit school library to select reading for DEAR time.

3:00 – 3:30 **Class Meeting/Dismissal**
Discussion of day's activities and future class plans.

Though they have set schedules, the teachers are flexible about adapting them to students' needs and to teachable moments.

Writing Resources

It's important to support students as participants in shared writing activities and to have resources within the classroom that enable them to become writers. We include the following resources as a necessary part of any primary writing classroom.

✳ Alphabet Chart

Centre Ridge and Halley teachers look for alphabet charts that include the upper and lower case versions of each letter and a familiar picture beginning with its sound. They usually post the chart near the shared writing area, so students can easily refer to it. Students are given a smaller version of the chart, so they'll have correct, consistent sound/letter symbols to support their independent writing. This small alphabet chart is usually taped to the student's desk or placed in a writing folder.

Coordinate with other teachers to use the same alphabet chart so that students have a consistent letter/symbol association for kindergarten through second grade.

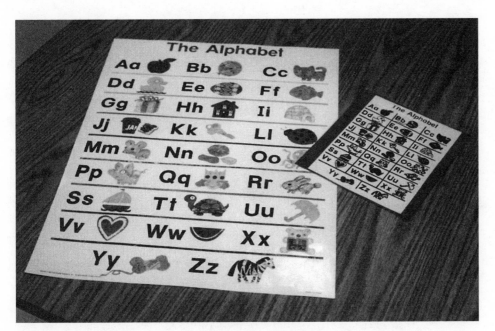

Typical alphabet charts used by Centre Ridge and Halley teachers and students.

First grade teacher Amy Dux likes to design an alphabet chart with her students. After reading many alphabet books, Amy and her first graders create a class alphabet wall chart. Later, they make a desk chart, and big book and small book versions of their class alphabet, which provides Amy's students with multiple opportunities to become familiar with letters and sounds.

Amy Dux's first graders created their own class alphabet chart.

Tip Box

How to Create
an Alphabet Wall Chart

- Use a large piece of butcher paper (36" x 56").

- Divide the paper into sections, 7 rows across, each 8" wide, and 4 columns down, each 9" deep.

- Place the letters in alphabetical order going across (two boxes will remain empty in row 4).

- Select a picture with the class to represent each letter. Consider using student illustrations, pictures from magazines, or computer-created pictures. Let students use newspapers and magazines to go on a scavenger hunt to find letters presented in a variety of fonts. Paste the pictures and letters in the appropriate boxes.

- Label each picture on the chart with its name.

Our teachers plan ways to acquaint students with the alphabet chart. Recently Carleen, in her resource teacher role, visited Patty Cruzan's kindergarten classroom and demonstrated how to use the chart.

Mrs. Payne: I hear /m/ at the beginning of *monkey*. What letter makes the /m/ sound? Let's look at our alphabet chart to see which picture starts like *monkey*. *Cat? Fish? Mouse?*

Sonja: *Mouse.*

Mrs. Payne: Let me say *mouse* and *monkey* slowly. Listen to the beginning sounds while I say the words. *Mouse. Monkey.* Yes, *mouse* starts like *monkey*. I'll trace the *m* with my finger, so I can write the letter the correct way.

Carrie Campbell, a first grade teacher, frequently begins her shared reading with an alphabet warm-up. She and her students read, sing, or chant the alphabet chart to build familiarity with the sound/letter symbols. Carrie is helping her students learn to quickly associate letters with their sounds.

Carrie: (points and chants) *A, a, apple; B, b, balloon; C, c, cat...*

Carrie cautions: Include only the name of the letter and the word that it begins with in alphabet-chart chants. Adding extra words—for example, *A, a is for a big apple*—confuses students.

❋ Names Chart

In *Becoming Literate*, Marie Clay states, "The use of the children's names in a class activity is a useful way of developing letter knowledge." Since most children come to school knowing their names, many of our teachers create wall displays of students' names. They write names on tag board sentence strips, construction paper, or chart paper. Some also include a picture of each student.

Linda Bowlin begins by writing her first graders' first names on brightly colored paper. She organizes the names alphabetically under her chalkboard near the shared writing area at a comfortable height for her students. She uses the student names for a variety of learning activities—in shared writing stories, nursery rhymes, poems or songs. For example, she might do a shared writing adaptation of "Jack be Nimble":

Nicole
Nicole be nimble, Nicole be quick.
Nicole jump over the candlestick.

Linda shows her first graders how to use their names as a way to connect to a beginning sound of a word when she is writing.

Mrs. Bowlin: *Jump starts like James, Janelle, and Jason.*

Linda Bowlin uses her name wall for a variety of writing activities.

For kindergartners and first graders, create a class alphabet big book with student names as the key word for every letter you can. Include the upper- and lower-case versions of the letter for each page of the book. You can use the alphabet big book as a writing resource during shared writing activities.

S is for Scott and other s words in Terry Creamer's first grade class alphabet book.

❋ Word Wall

A word wall is a place in the classroom to display high-frequency words. These should be the words the teacher and students use repeatedly. You'll find some high-frequency word lists in Donald Graves' book, *A Fresh Look at Writing*, and in Patricia Cunningham's book, *Phonics We Use*. The word walls in Centre Ridge and Halley classrooms encourage an interest in words, help students develop a common bank of words for writing, provide an opportunity to view words in another setting, and promote an awareness that words have a correct spelling.

The word wall in Terry Creamer's first grade starts with student names.

Word walls are different in kindergarten, first grade, and second grade classrooms. During the school year, Katie Abruzzino, a kindergarten teacher, builds a list of about 20 high-frequency words that she and her students discover during their shared reading time. Katie writes these words on sentence strips, glues magnetic strips behind the words, and places them on her chalkboard. When Katie or her kindergartners are engaged in shared writing, they frequently check the chalkboard for familiar words. Katie says she's not concerned about her kindergartners learning lots of words but rather wants to be sure that they learn a few very important words. If you peeked in her room, you'd see such words as *like, the, my, is, mom, dad,* and *and* on her chalkboard.

Tip Box

Word Wall Suggestions

- Place the word wall near the shared writing area, if possible.
- Choose words that students will meet frequently in their reading and writing.
- Create a climate that promotes an interest in words.
- Arrange words in alphabetical order.
- Encourage students to contribute words.
- Designate time to review, add, or delete words.
- Illustrate words where appropriate.
- Plan the height of the word wall so students can use it.
- Demonstrate how to use the word wall during shared writing activities.

Pamela Mahoney and her first graders begin to build their word wall in the first few weeks of school. They start by creating a chart for each letter of the alphabet. Pamela and the students discuss how they'll make the letters for each chart and what order they'll put the letters in when they hang up the charts. Pamela says, "I want my students to have the sense that this word wall belongs to them! My favorite time with the word wall is at the beginning of the school year, when everyone gets to put his name up on the wall. We have more conversations about the alphabet, letter order, and letter formation. My first graders are getting their first experience with words, and it starts with the alphabet and their names!"

After students have placed their names on the word wall, Pamela uses the daily morning message to help students discover some of the high-frequency words they see in print and use in their writing. Following the writing of the morning message with her first graders, Pamela's conversation goes something like this:

Ms. Mahoney: Let's read our morning message together.

Good morning first graders!

We will have music.

Officer Oliver will visit.

It will be a fun day.

I noticed that we have a word in our morning message that we have seen in our reading and a word we use a lot in our writing. We used it three times in our message today. Who can find that word?

Sarah:	I think it's *will*.
Ms. Mahoney:	Yes, it's *will*. Will is a word we often see in our writing. Say it slowly with me, *w-i-ll*. How many sounds do you hear?
Maria:	Three, but I see four letters.
Ms. Mahoney:	We do hear three sounds but we write four letters. There are two *l*'s in *will*. Let's circle the word *will* in our morning message. Jose, can you circle *will* for us?
	(Jose circles *will* three times.)
Ms. Mahoney:	*Will* is a word we frequently see in our reading and writing, so we can put it on our word wall. Sarah, would you like to write the word *will* on this card? We'll put *will* on our word wall. Then when we're not sure how to write it, we'll be able to check the word wall.

Pamela and her first graders frequently find the words for their word wall in the daily morning message. Pamela's students see a connection between the words they read and write. If you walked into Pamela's room during writer's workshop, you'd notice some of her first graders looking up at the word wall to find the words they need to spell.

Molly Connolly's second graders come in knowing many high-frequency words, but they don't often bother to check out how to spell them correctly. The word wall in Molly's room is a resource for her students.

Molly says, "Our classroom word wall provides a way for me to hold students accountable for spelling high-frequency words correctly as well as to extend students' knowledge of words. By the time my students leave second grade, I want them to know how to spell words like *they, love,* and *what* and be able to use some of the common homophones such as *to, two,* and *too* correctly. We also use our word wall to learn about how words work. For example, if my students know how to spell *look,* I want them to know that they can spell *looks, looking,* and *looked.*"

Molly frequently helps students select words for their word wall from science and social studies units. She says, "My second graders will come across the same words when they are doing a science unit and will need to spell them again and again. That's when we decide to put these words on our wall! For example, when we were hatching chicks as part of our science unit, you'd have seen such words as *rooster, egg,* and *chicken* on our wall. When we finished the chick unit, we made a "chick" dictionary and put it in our writing reference area. My second graders have enjoyed reading that dictionary and a few of the others we've made."

As your word wall begins to grow, it's important to model its use during shared writing activities so that your students will refer to it when they write independently. Carleen did this when she went into Pamela Mahoney's classroom for a shared writing activity.

Mrs. Payne:	I need to write the word *cute*. It has a /k/ sound. It could start with the letter *k* or *c*.
Josie:	It's under the *c*. It starts with a *c* and has the letters *c-u-t*.
Mrs. Payne:	You're almost right, Josie, but *c-u-t* is *cut*. *Cute* has an *e* on the end. Do you see a word like that on the word wall?

| Josie: | Yes, it's next to *cookie*. |
| Mrs. Payne: | Both of these words, *cut* and *cute* look almost the same. We'll need to remember that *cute* has an *e* on the end. |

Once your word wall is established, use extension activities to help build students' knowledge about written language. Here are a few to try.

• *word sorts to categorize words*

Mrs. Payne:	Let's make a list of the words on our word wall that belong to the *u-n* word pattern, like *fun*.
Stacey:	I see *run* under the *r* words.
Don:	*Sun* is in the *s* words.
Mrs. Payne:	If I know how to write *fun*, then I also know how to write *sun*, because *fun* and *sun* end the same way with the *u-n* pattern.

Word sorts can include: letter(s); sound(s); syllables; affixes; topics.

• *word displays highlighting content-area vocabulary*

For a study of nutrition, for example, student words may include *fruits, vegetables, vitamins*, and so on.

Terry Creamer's first graders brainstormed a list of nutrition words and facts. ▶

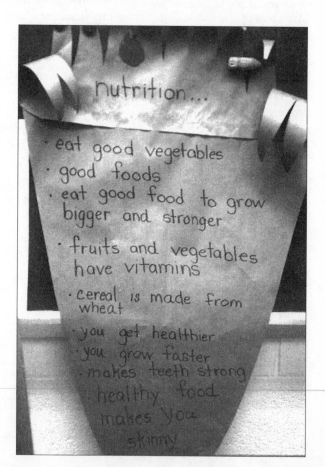

• *discuss concepts about print to call attention to key concepts*

Mrs. Schulman:	Who can find a word with a capital letter?
Gen:	Ryan has a capital R.
Mrs. Schulman:	Who can find a word that starts and ends with the same letter?
Margo:	I think *dad* starts and ends with a *d*.
Mrs. Schulman:	How do you know?
Margo:	I see a *d* at the beginning and end of the word.
Mrs. Schulman:	You're right, Margo. There's a *d* at the beginning and end of the word *dad*.

❋ Reference Materials

Shared writing presents an excellent opportunity for primary-level students to learn why and how to use reference books. As resource teachers, we help Centre Ridge and Halley teachers select classroom reference books that are up-to-date and easy for primary students to use. We try to choose paperback versions which, because they're less costly, permits regular replacement. Our choices include a variety of children's picture and junior dictionaries, a children's encyclopedia, a thesaurus, a rhyming dictionary, an atlas, and a writer's reference book. See the Appendix for specific suggestions.

Some of the reference books found in Halley and Centre Ridge classrooms.

During shared writing, we encourage the use of reference materials by demonstrating how to use a particular type as a source of information. For example, here's how we model the use of a picture dictionary:

Mrs. Payne: We'll be writing the word *dinosaur* many times in our story. Let's look it up in our picture dictionary so that we can spell it correctly. Where should I look?

Michael: Under the *d*'s.

Mrs. Payne: How do you know?

Michael: Because *dinosaur* starts with the letter *d*.

Mrs. Payne: Will that be near the beginning, the middle, or end of the dictionary?

John: Near the beginning, because *d* is near the beginning of the alphabet.

*I*n this chapter we've discussed a classroom environment that is conducive to shared writing. We've focused on a balanced literacy program, the classroom organization, the materials, and the management of shared writing. As you establish your classroom environment, consider these questions:

❋ Are reading and writing seen as purposeful activities?
❋ Are students invited to participate in organizing the classroom?
❋ Is there time for students to work on writing as a class, a group, and individually?
❋ Do all students have opportunities to succeed in writing?
❋ Are the writing resources available to beginning writers meaningful, relevant, and useful?

Getting the most Out of
Morning Message,
Daily News, and the
Class Message

> "Writing is learned by writing, by reading, and perceiving oneself as a writer..."
>
> —Frank Smith,
> Writing and the Writer

It's 8:50 a.m. in Terry Creamer's first grade classroom. Twenty-seven students are gathered at Terry's feet on the rug in front of the easel ready to begin the day with the class morning meeting. During their meeting, the students and Terry routinely compose a morning message together using an easel, newsprint, chart paper, or the computer. The morning message is brief, no more than two to six sentences. Topics are based on recent or upcoming school or class events—a memorable incident, an anticipated field trip, or something a student or Terry wants to share.

Crystal helps write the morning message in Terry Creamer's first grade classroom.

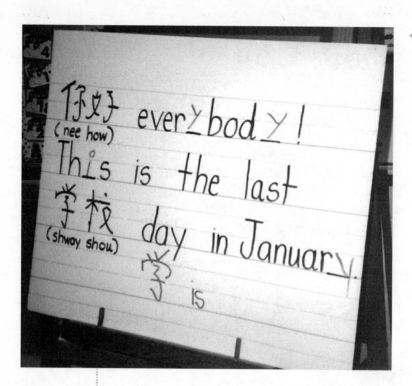

Terry Creamer and her first graders' morning message included Chinese characters when they were studying modern-day China. The first graders quickly figured out that the characters represented the words "hello" and "school" by reading and drawing on the meaning of the rest of the message. Terry linked this technique to DEAR time. She pointed out how the students might try thinking about the meaning of what they're reading, and what would make sense if they came across unknown or tricky words.

Early in the school year, Terry does most of the writing. She sometimes starts with a portion of the message already written and then asks questions that lead students to suggest additions. Together, she and her students share in writing the new part. Individual students write the parts they know or can figure out with help, and Terry writes the parts that they've yet to learn. The marker moves naturally back and forth between the students' hands and Terry's hand until the message is complete. During the year, as students gain knowledge of letter sounds, words, and how written language works, they need less help, and they write more and more of the morning message themselves.

Terry accomplishes a great deal of teaching about writing during the 10–20 minutes spent composing the morning message with the first graders. She demonstrates the purposes writing can serve, concepts about print, how to hear sounds in words, the options writers have, and the strategies writers use. She says, "I'm making visible the things kids need to know about writing—the same things I want them to consider doing or using when they write on their own in their journals, learning logs or during writing workshop."

Writing a morning message, daily news, or class message with students is a powerful way for teachers to demonstrate how writing works and to help students cross the bridge to independent writing. Here are a few ways you can involve kindergartners, and first and second graders in writing the morning message, daily news or class message.

☑ *Help students create the text for a message.*

Carleen: (in a first grade classroom) Jenna told us about her new bike and how she plans to ride it over the weekend. What are some of the rest of you doing? Have you been thinking about what we might write in the morning message today?

Mary: (in a second grade classroom) Today is Secretary Appreciation Day. How might we include ideas about that in our Halley morning message? Yes, we could make a list of ways the secretaries help us. Okay, let's keep that in mind. Who else has an idea?

☑ *Have students decide about print conventions.*

Carleen: (in a first grade classroom) What letter will you write first in your name? Will you use an uppercase or a lowercase S? Why? That's right, we begin people's names with capital letters.

Mary: (in a second grade classroom) Which *to* will you write? How *do* you know it should be *t-w-o*? That's right. We mean the number *two*.

☑ *Prompt students to hear sounds in words when they write.*

Mary: (in a kindergarten classroom) Okay, Kinders, let's say *today* slowly and listen for the sounds we can hear in *today*. (Students and teacher slowly articulate *TOOODAAA(Y)*.) What do you hear first? Who can write the first part?

☑ *Share the pen with students to write the message.*

Mary: (in a first grade classroom) Help us with your name, Deon. Where will you write your name in the message? That's right. You see that there's room to write it at the end of this line. And it'll be easy to read because you've left a space.

Carleen: (in a second grade classroom) Clap the word *information*. What's the first part? Kevin, write *in*, the first part you heard. Let's clap again. What part do we hear next? Shardae added *for*, so now we have *in-for*. Let's clap again to hear what the next part is (students and teacher clap *in-for-ma-tion*). What's the next part? That's right, */ma/*. Candice write that part. Now let's clap to see what we hear last. You're right, Cole. It sounds like it should be *s-h-u-n*, but let me show you how we write that last part */tion/* at the end of *information*. We write it *t-i-o-n*. Do you see how that looks? It doesn't look the way it sounds, does it?

☑ *Have students experience some of the processes that are important to writing independently.*

Mary:	(in a first grade classroom) Miguel, where are you going to write the word *the*? Why are you going to put *the* there? That's right. There's no room on this line. Look what Miguel did. He went back over here on this line, because there was no more room to write up here. Now, let's read what we have so far.
Carleen:	(in a kindergarten classroom) What do I need to remember to leave before I write the next word? That's right. Spaces between words makes it easier for us to read. Let's reread to see what we've written so far. Did you see how rereading what we wrote helped us figure out that the next word we need is *and*?

Guiding the Daily News in Kindergarten

Each morning Gina Bangert and her students gather for opening circle time. Here they connect to one another through the daily rituals and routines and conversational sharing. They sing a greeting, read and incorporate calendar activities, complete a weather-report chart, chant a finger play or rhyme, and share in writing the daily news. The daily news is usually two to four sentences long and frequently includes information about the students. Gina says, "I like writing about the kids in the daily news because it provides lots of opportunities to use their names. That way they can contribute to the writing early on just by writing their names."

On this day early in the school year, Gina and the students write about what they were doing and where they're going over the upcoming weekend.

◀ *Kindergartners in Gina Bangert's class share in writing the daily news when they write their names.*

Ms. Bangert:	Now that we know what we're going to write about, it's time for...
Students:	...the kindergarten news. (*Gina writes* Kindergarten News *on the chart, then points and reads it.*)
Ms. Bangert:	Now, what should I write first?
Anas:	*Friday.*
Lena:	*Today is Friday.*
Ms. Bangert:	Okay, let's write all of that. Who can show me where we begin writing? (*Jon comes up and points to the top, left.*) That's right. Show me which way I should write. (*Jon indicates from left to right.*) You know how writing goes in the news, don't you, Jon? We always start here and write this way (*pointing and indicating left-to-right*). Who can tell us what *today* starts with? Let's say it slowly first and listen for the sounds we can hear in the word *today*. (*Gina and the students slowly articulate* TOOODAAAA(Y).) What do you hear first?
Carla:	*T.*
Ms. Bangert:	That's right. *Today* starts like *turtle* on the alphabet chart. Where should I write the *T*? (*Carla points to the beginning of the line on the chart paper*). Carla, can you write the *T*?
Carla:	I forgot how.
Ms. Bangert:	Let's check the alphabet chart. Trace the *T* with your finger. I'll help. It's a line down and a line on top. Now you hold the marker, and I'll help you make the *T* for *today*. Now, let's say *today* again slowly. *TOOODAAAA(Y)*. What else do you hear?
Kim:	*A.*
Ben:	*D.*
Ms. Bangert:	You're both right. But first we'll need to write *o*, then the *d* and now the *a*. Then there's another letter you can't hear, it's a *y*. (*Gina writes the letters in the appropriate order stretching the word out slowly as she writes it.*) Now, say the word *today* slowly one more time with me. Watch as I point. (*The students and Gina stretch out* today *again while she slides her finger under the word at the same time.*) What will we write next?
Jimmy:	*Is.*
Ms. Bangert:	Before I write *is*, what do I need to remember to do?
Chip:	Leave a space.
Ms. Bangert:	That's right. Spaces make it easier for us to read. Remember how they left spaces in the book we read yesterday about Humpty Dumpty? Now watch while I write *is*. (*Gina says* is *slowly as she writes the word.*) Okay, let's read what we have so far, *Today is....* (*Gina points as they read.*) What comes next?
Kate:	*Friday.*

Ms. Bangert: Kate, what will I need to do before I write *Friday*? That's right. I need to leave a space again. How will I begin *Friday*? That's right, Daniel—an F. Watch while I write *Friday*. (Gina writes *Friday* and says it slowly, matching the letter sound with the letter.) Now let's read. (The class reads as Gina points to the words. Gina and the students share in writing the rest of the daily news. Sally, Carlos, Matt and Jenna help by writing their names.)

Gina says, "At the beginning of the school year, I'm helping the kids realize that what they think and say can be written down. Early on, we work on concepts about print such as where to start writing, left-to-right, top-to-bottom, return sweep, and spacing. I help them learn how to say words slowly and listen for sounds. I support them by writing what they can't write yet. As the year progresses, students write more of the high-frequency words such as *the, I, we, go, is*, and *like* themselves. They learn to hear most beginning-letter sounds, many ending-letter sounds, and even some medial-letter sounds. We talk about when to use punctuation and capital and lowercase letters. When the students write on their own in journals or at the writing center, I can refer back to things we've talked about while writing the daily news. Keeping to the ritual of writing the daily news helps me to keep extending the students' learning."

The visual text on the next page shows other possibilities for teaching during shared writing of the daily news. When Gina plans what she'll focus on in the daily news, she thinks about how to help her students with what they can't quite do in their own writing. She plans her instruction on what the students can do and stretches them just a little.

Sally Murray's kindergarten students read the morning messages notebook during DEAR time. Each day, after she and the class write their message on the chalkboard, Sally types it. Then a student illustrates it, and it's added to the notebook. ▶

Teaching Possibilities:
A Kindergarten Class' Shared Writing
of the Daily News

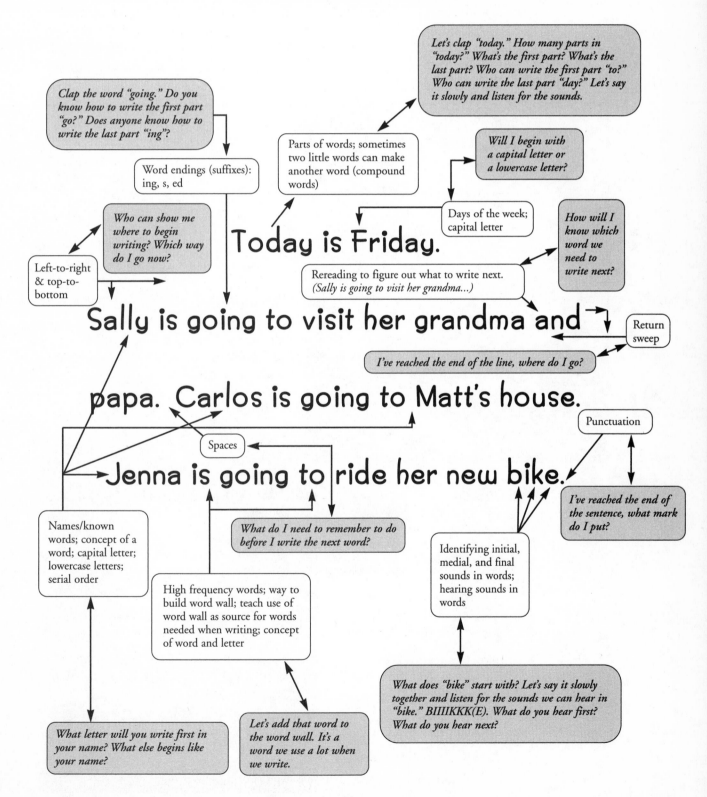

Guiding the Morning Message in First Grade

Let's revisit Terry Creamer's first grade classroom during the shared writing of the morning message. Terry begins by reading and pointing to the first sentence she put on the chart before school. Then she and the students read the sentence aloud. They talk about the day's events and about other ideas they'll add to the message.

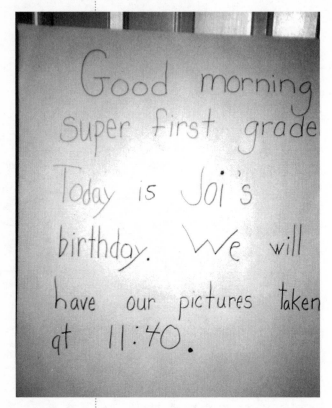

◀ *First graders share the pen with teacher Terry Creamer to write the morning message.*

Mrs. Creamer:	We decided the next part we're going to write is *Today is Joi's birthday.* What will we write first?
Jeff:	*Today.*
Mrs. Creamer:	That's a good word to clap. Let's clap *today.* What do you hear first?
Carley:	*To.*
Mrs. Creamer:	Let's clap *today* again and listen for what we hear next.
Lee:	*Day.*
Mrs. Creamer:	Who can write the first part, *to?* Okay, Carley, before you start tell us how you'll begin.
Carley:	With a *t.*
Mrs. Creamer:	Yes, that's right, but will you use a capital *T* or a lowercase *t* when you write the first part *to?*
Carley:	A capital *T.*
Mrs. Creamer:	Why will you use a capital *T?*

Carley:	It's the first letter—no—the first word in the sentence.
Mrs. Creamer:	Yes, *Today* is the first word in the sentence, and we make the first letter a capital to show this. Now write that first part for us. (Carley writes *To*.)
Mrs. Creamer:	Lee says the next part is *day*. Let's say it slowly and listen for the sounds we hear. (Terry and the students say *daaaaa(y)*.) Can you hear some of the sounds in that part? Good. But let's try to figure out how to write that word another way. I'm going to give you a clue. We know another word that has the same pattern as *day*. The word is *play*. We could look for *play* on the word wall, but I want you to look here. (Terry writes *play* on a whiteboard.) Think how we can make *play* into *day*. What part would we change?
Paul:	*P* to a *d*.
Mrs. Creamer:	Let's try it. Watch while I write it the way Paul says we should write it. (Terry writes *dlay* on the whiteboard.) Now, read it with me slowly to check. (Terry slides her finger under the *dlay* slowly as they read together.) Does it sound right—*dlllaaaa(y)*?
Jenny:	No. It needs to be *d-a-y*. Take the *l* away.
Mrs. Creamer:	Watch while I write it the way Jenny says we should write it. (Terry writes *day* on the whiteboard.) Now read it with me slowly to check. (Terry slides her finger under the word slowly as they read *day* together.) Does that sound right—*day*? Okay, it sounds right. Now let's check to see if it looks right. Does it have the same pattern as *play*? What's the pattern?
Sarah:	*A-y*.
Mrs. Creamer:	Who else thinks the pattern is *a-y*? (Students raise hands.) You really checked. Watch while I write both words. See how they're the same? (Terry points to the pattern *a-y* in each word.) Now, here is a thinking question. Where is the pattern the same—at the beginning, middle, or end of the word?
Patrick:	At the end… no, at the middle and end.
Mrs. Creamer:	Let's look again and check to see if Patrick is right. (Terry points to the middle and end of the word.) First grade thinkers, you're coming up with different ways to figure out words to write! Sometimes you say them slowly and listen for the sounds. And just now you used a word you know to figure out how to write another word like it. Now, let's add *day* to the message. (Patrick writes *day* on the message.) Let's read what we have so far. (Terry points as she and the students read from the beginning of the message.) What word do we need next?
Zachary:	*Is*.
Mrs. Creamer:	Yes. We need *is*. But before we write *is*, what do we need to remember to leave?
James:	A space.

Mrs. Creamer:	That's right. Leaving spaces between words when we write makes it easier for us to read. Who can write *is*? (Zachary writes *is*.)
	If we didn't know how to write *is*, what might we do?
Miguel:	Ask a friend.
Alex:	Say it slowly and listen for the sounds.
Mrs. Creamer:	Those are two good ideas. What else?
Crystal:	Think of another word like it that we know.
Mrs. Creamer:	Do you know another word like *is*, Crystal?
Crystal:	Yes, *in*.
Mrs. Creamer:	So tell us how you would figure out how to write *is* from *in*.
Crystal:	I'd say, You know how to write *in*... and *is* starts like *in* with an *i*...and I can hear the sound of *n* at the end.
Mrs. Creamer:	So, you were thinking about what you already know, about patterns in words, and about what letter sounds you hear...lots of good thinking. Does anyone have another way to figure out how to write *is*?
LaDonna:	Look on the word wall.
Mrs. Creamer:	That's right. The word wall has words we use a lot when writing. Let's check to see if *is* is on the word wall. Where should we look?
Brandon:	On the *i* list. (The students and Terry check and find the word *is* on the *i* list.)
Mrs. Creamer:	Brandon, how did you know we had to check the *i* list?
Brandon:	'Cause *is* starts with *i*.
Mrs. Creamer:	Thinking about how a word begins helps us know where to look on the word wall chart, doesn't it? Now, let's reread what we have so far, so we know what we should write next. (Terry points, and together they read the message from the beginning again.)
Mrs. Creamer:	The next word we need is...
Joi:	*Joi's*.
Mrs. Creamer:	Who do you think knows how to write that word?
First graders:	Joi!
Mrs. Creamer:	Help us with your name, Joi. Where will you write it in our message? (Joi points to the place on the chart, then writes her name.) We need to add something because we want to say *Joi's* instead of *Joi*. What do we need to add?
Julia:	An *s*.
Mrs. Creamer:	Yes, an *s*, but we also have to put this mark called an apostrophe before the *s*. We use an apostrophe *s* to help the reader know the birthday is *Joi's*. Later, we'll learn more about how to use apostrophes. Now let's read the message again so we'll know what word comes next. (The students and Terry read the message again as she points to the words.) What word comes next?

Briana:	*Birthday.*
Mrs. Creamer:	This is another good word to clap. Clap with me. (The students and Terry clap *birth—day*). What's the first part?
Alex:	*Birth.*
Mrs. Creamer:	What's the next part?
Emily:	*Day.*
Mrs. Creamer:	Let's say the first part slowly to see what sounds we can hear in *birth*. (Terry and the students say BBBIRRRRTHHH.) What will we write first? (Terry writes, as the students tell her the letter sounds in *birth*. She fills in the letter *i*, the only letter they don't know.) Emily said the next part is *day*. What can help you write the part *day*?
Todd:	Look up there where we wrote it before. (Todd indicates *Today* in the message.)
Mrs. Creamer:	Yes. If we can't remember a word we already used in our writing, we can go back and find it to see how to write it. (Terry and her students continue to move through the completion of the morning message together.)

Like many teachers at Halley and Centre Ridge who make the morning message a part of their instruction, Terry bases the skills and strategies she teaches on close observation of the learners in her classroom. She knows that she can accomplish a lot of teaching with a morning message, but she emphasizes that students really learn to write by writing on their own. "My students write almost every day in writing workshop," she says. "I look at what they write, and when I notice the same patterns in the students' writing, I know what strategy or skill to focus on in the morning message.

"I've found that I have to revisit things a lot. Teaching a skill once in the morning message doesn't mean the children have it. For example, I focused on spacing between words in many of our morning messages at the beginning of the year. Now, spacing comes naturally for the children, so we don't talk about it anymore. We've moved on to other things. The focus keeps changing as their own writing shows what they need to learn. In recent morning messages, we focused on how a writer can say the same thing in different ways, word meanings, word order, phonics, spelling, forms of writing—the list goes on. The fun part is seeing what you've modeled in the morning message appear in the children's independent writing—or seeing them notice it in something they're reading."

Now take a closer look at the visual text of the morning message Terry Creamer wrote with her first graders to get an idea of some of the other teaching possibilities.

Teaching Possibilities:
A First Grade Class' Shared Writing
of the Morning Message

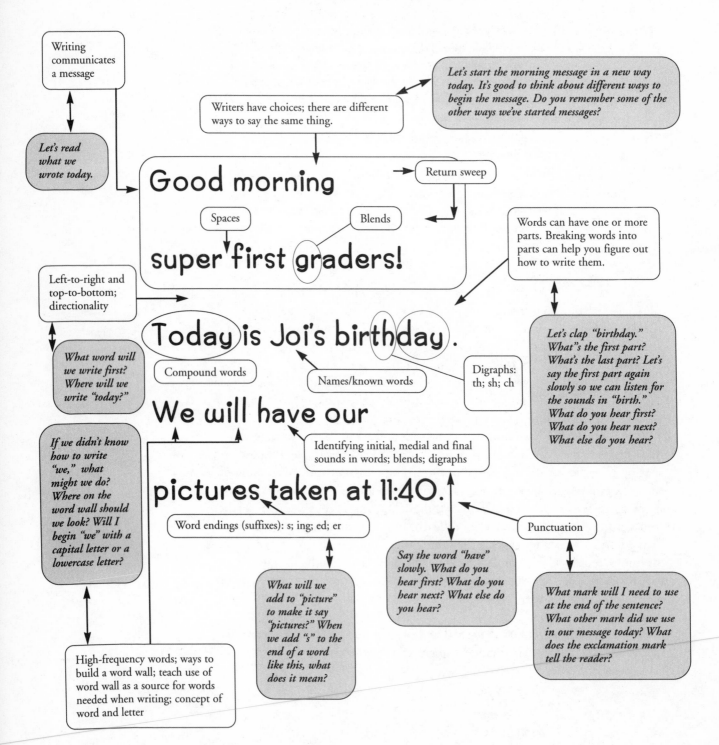

Writing communicates a message

Let's read what we wrote today.

Writers have choices; there are different ways to say the same thing.

Let's start the morning message in a new way today. It's good to think about different ways to begin the message. Do you remember some of the other ways we've started messages?

Good morning

Return sweep

Spaces

Blends

super first graders!

Words can have one or more parts. Breaking words into parts can help you figure out how to write them.

Left-to-right and top-to-bottom; directionality

Today is Joi's birthday.

Compound words

Names/known words

Digraphs: th; sh; ch

Let's clap "birthday." What"s the first part? What's the last part? Let's say the first part again slowly so we can listen for the sounds in "birth." What do you hear first? What do you hear next? What else do you hear?

What word will we write first? Where will we write "today?"

We will have our

Identifying initial, medial and final sounds in words; blends; digraphs

If we didn't know how to write "we," what might we do? Where on the word wall should we look? Will I begin "we" with a capital letter or a lowercase letter?

pictures taken at 11:40.

Word endings (suffixes): s; ing; ed; er

Punctuation

Say the word "have" slowly. What do you hear first? What do you hear next? What else do you hear?

What will we add to "picture" to make it say "pictures?" When we add "s" to the end of a word like this, what does it mean?

What mark will I need to use at the end of the sentence? What other mark did we use in our message today? What does the exclamation mark tell the reader?

High-frequency words; ways to build a word wall; teach use of word wall as a source for words needed when writing; concept of word and letter

Guiding a Class Message in Second Grade

Two or three times a week, Molly Connolly and her second graders can be seen huddling around the overhead projector to write a class message. Molly uses the activity as a warm-up to her writing workshop session. Like the daily news Gina Bangert writes with her kindergartners and the morning message Terry Creamer writes with her first graders, Molly's shared writing of the class message offers a range of teaching opportunities.

Molly says, "The class message often relates to what we're studying in language arts, science, social studies, math, or health. For example, the day before we went on a field trip to the zoo, the class message was about that. Early in the year, I give the students topic ideas that relate to what we're studying, but it's not long before they begin to think and plan ahead for what we might write. When we were studying poetry as a genre, we wrote a class poem. When we were talking about double numbers in math, we wrote math problems with double numbers.

"Writing about subjects we're studying helps narrow the possible topics we might write about, leads to discussions that help clarify and review some of what the children are learning, widens the range of vocabulary we use, and contributes words to our word wall. I've noticed that at this level my students already know how to write many of the high-frequency words. Those are words I automatically write when they appear in the class message. Instead, the words I focus on are usually words the students almost have under control in their writing or are just good words to analyze to learn how language works. Writing a class message with the students a few times a week is a great way to lift up the their learning."

Here is a part of the exchange between Molly and her second graders as they write a class message.

Mrs. Connolly:	You're right , Robb. Researching has three parts. How will you write the first part?
Robb:	*R-e.*
Mrs. Connolly:	What's the next part?
Eileen:	*Search.*
Mrs. Connolly:	How will you write it? (Eileen writes *serch.*) That's a good try. You're almost right, but there's a silent letter in there. What letter do you think might go in there, and where would you put it? Eileen want to give it a try?
Eileen:	I think an *a,* but I'm not sure where.
Mrs. Connolly:	Anthony thinks he can help us out.
Anthony:	After the *e.* (Anthony adds the *a* where it belongs.)
Mrs. Connolly:	Now, so far we have *research,* do we need anything else?
Joshua:	Yes, *i-n-g,* /ing/. (Joshua adds *i-n-g.*)

Mrs. Connolly:	Now, look at *researching*. Check to see if you see a word within that word? What is it?
Beth:	*Search.*
Mrs. Connolly:	Do you know what we call that part of the word?
Kristi:	I think it's a root word.
Mrs. Connolly:	Exactly. We can take some words and add to the beginning of them and to the ending of them to make a new word. Does anyone know what we call the part we add or fix to the beginning, like *re* in *researching*?
Gene:	A blend.
Mrs. Connolly:	Why *do* you think it's a blend?
Gene:	Because the two sounds blend together when you say it.
Mrs. Connolly:	That's good thinking, but the blending of the sounds doesn't have anything to do with this. When we add something on to the beginning of a word like *search*, we call it a prefix. Say that word with me. (Molly and the students say *prefix*.) Let's clap it. Do you hear that first part *pre*? *Pre* means first or before. Let's clap it again. Hear the last part *fix*? *Fix* means to attach it or add it. So it might help to think of *prefix* like this. You fix it to the first part of a root word. Just like *re* was fixed to the first part of *search* to make *research*. Anyone else have a way to think about the meaning of the word *prefix*?
MaryAnne:	You could think about it like adding to the front part of the word. Like we added *re* to the front part of *search*.

Molly and her second grade students' dialogue while writing the class message continued with a discussion of word endings and the suffixes they already knew how to use in their writing. When they finished writing the class message, Molly and her students reread it together to check their writing.

Molly uses the class message to teach her students the importance of rereading what they've written. She models how to reread slowly after writing something to make sure it makes sense, and she shows students how to check to see if they need to add or change something in the writing. She explains, "I'd noticed that the writing students brought to a writing workshop conference with me usually contained careless errors and omissions that I thought they should have caught on their own through rereading. But as I conferred with students, I realized that they weren't rereading properly. They didn't realize that, in order to reread to check and confirm their writing, they would have to read slowly, not fluently."

Now take a closer look at some of the other teaching possibilities Molly might have with a class message.

Teaching Possibilities:
A Second Grade Class' Shared Writing
of a Class Message

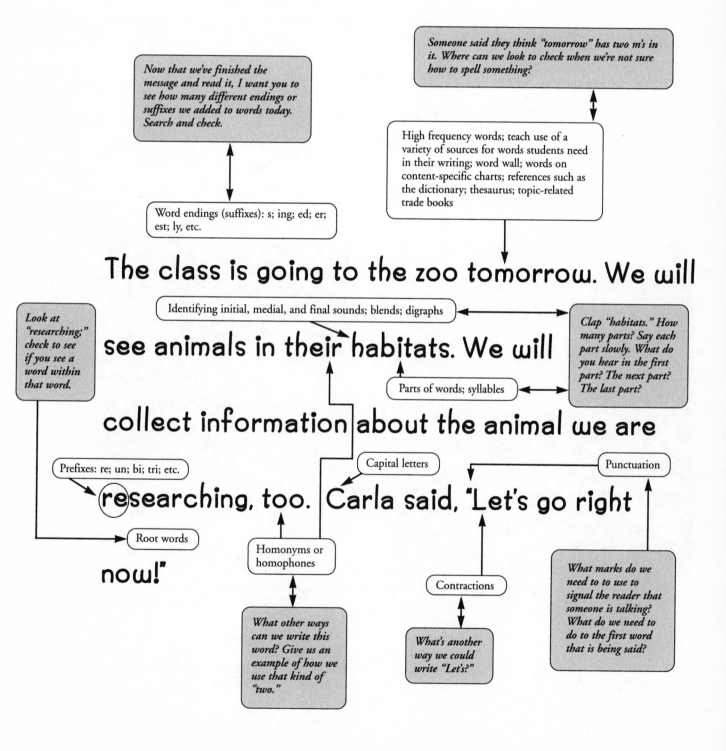

Now that we've finished the message and read it, I want you to see how many different endings or suffixes we added to words today. Search and check.

Someone said they think "tomorrow" has two m's in it. Where can we look to check when we're not sure how to spell something?

High frequency words; teach use of a variety of sources for words students need in their writing; word wall; words on content-specific charts; references such as the dictionary; thesaurus; topic-related trade books

Word endings (suffixes): s; ing; ed; er; est; ly, etc.

The class is going to the zoo tomorrow. We will

Look at "researching;" check to see if you see a word within that word.

Identifying initial, medial, and final sounds; blends; digraphs

Clap "habitats." How many parts? Say each part slowly. What do you hear in the first part? The next part? The last part?

see animals in their habitats. We will

Parts of words; syllables

collect information about the animal we are

Prefixes: re; un; bi; tri; etc.

Capital letters

Punctuation

researching, too. Carla said, "Let's go right

Root words

Homonyms or homophones

Contractions

What marks do we need to to use to signal the reader that someone is talking? What do we need to do to the first word that is being said?

now!"

What other ways can we write this word? Give us an example of how we use that kind of "two."

What's another way we could write "Let's?"

Morning Message Extensions

Once you and your students have composed and reread the morning message, you may want to return to the message or news to do one or two of the following:

- Search and locate a few letters, words, or sentences (circle with marker or use Wikki Stix™).
- Look for print conventions (capital letters, punctuation, spacing).
- Clap words for parts (What's the first part? Second part?).
- Select a word from the message and brainstorm other words that begin or end the same way (consonants, vowels, blends, digraphs, etc.).
- Generate other words with the same pattern as a word in the message (use magnetic letters or a whiteboard).

▲ *First grader Anthony writes his own list of words with patterns.*

◄ *After writing the morning message, Terry Creamer and the students generate a list of other words like the word* look, *which was in the message.*

- Link something from the shared writing to independent writing or reading time. *(We started the message with a question today. You could do that in your own writing sometime. Remember, when we didn't know what to write next, we reread what we had so far. You can do that when you write, too).*
- Reflect on using available resources to problem solve during shared writing *(When Cole didn't know how to make a* d, *where did he look to check?)*

*W*riting a morning message, daily news, or class message with students is a powerful way for teachers to demonstrate how writing works and to extend the students' participation during the school year.

Remember that one or two demonstrations of a skill or strategy are not enough; students need to be shown over and over again. You'll want to plan opportunities to explore, explain, and demonstrate many times during shared writing experiences such as the daily news, morning message, or the class message. Guide the students through composing, supporting them as they make decisions about what to write and how to write it. Ask questions, listen to responses, and acknowledge insights and learning. Students will not only learn from you, a more experienced writer; they'll learn from one another as you share the pen.

Literature as Models for Shared Writing

"We can read without ever having written, but we cannot write without having read."

—Andrea Butler & Jan Turbill, Towards a Reading-Writing Classroom

Above: Pamela Mahoney's first graders read the familiar rhyme "One, Two, Buckle My Shoe" during literacy center time.

Halley and Centre Ridge students are surrounded by stories, poems, and songs, because our teachers know that literature helps build many reading and writing skills. It also provides a familiar link to writing. Students begin to borrow the language of the books they've shared, organize their ideas in some of the same ways, and start to explore the different forms of writing.

In our work as resource teachers, we've found nursery rhymes, poems, songs, wordless books, and predictable stories to be invaluable models for shared writing. These shared writing experiences may include *innovations* on a text and written *retellings* of a familiar story.

An innovation might use the original story, poem, or rhyme as a model and change as little as one word in the text. For example, in Sarah Cobb's kindergarten classroom, Carleen and the kindergartners chose to rewrite "Jack and Jill." Students substituted their names for the character names in the rhyme.

Laurie and Scott

Laurie and Scott went up the hill,
To fetch a pail of water;
Scott fell down and broke his crown,
And Laurie came tumbling after.

Sometimes an innovation is a rewriting of a repetitive phrase or sentence. In Pamela Mahoney's first grade classroom, Carleen and the students chose to rewrite a repetitive sentence from the story, *The Three Little Pigs*.

"Then I'll **bump**, and I'll **jump**, and I'll **stomp** your house down," said the wolf to the first little pig...

Innovations may also involve using portions or most of a story's framework to make a completely new piece. Mary and a group of second graders from Molly Connolly's class read many Clifford stories and then decided to borrow parts from the book *Clifford, The Big Red Dog* to create a different version of the story. Here's a portion of their story:

Clifford Goes to Mars

Hi, I'm Annie and this is Jessica, Stephanie, and Meghan. This is our dog, Clifford. Clifford made a rocket. She went up to the planet Mars.

On the way to Mars, Clifford stopped at the zoo on the planet Pluto. She saw an alien zebra. She was scared of the zebra because it was as big as she was!

Sometimes we use shared writing to retell familiar tales, such as *The Gingerbread Man, Little Red Riding Hood,* or *Goldilocks and the Three Bears.* Since many of our students are familiar with the plots and know some of the story language, these tales serve as strong models. We write the retelling on chart paper or create it as a book.

◀ *Terry Creamer's first graders create their own version of "Breakfast in Bed."*

When we create innovations or retellings of the stories, poems, and songs we've enjoyed, we look for ways to share the pen with our students. We consider the writing development of the students and the writing skills we need to demonstrate. Sometimes we act as the scribe. At other times we have our students write portions of the text we know they can contribute.

Let's take a more detailed look at some of the ways we've created innovations and retellings in Centre Ridge and Halley classrooms.

Using Nursery Rhymes, Songs, and Poems With Kindergartners

Nursery rhymes, poems, and songs are brief, and they're familiar to most students. The predictability of the verses, the repetitive nature of the words and phrases, and the rhythm and rhyme are appealing. Here's a shared writing experience with nursery rhymes that we have tried in kindergarten. Carleen used it in two sessions with Sally Murray's class. You could substitute any familiar poem or song. You'll need:

- copy of the nursery rhyme "Little Miss Muffet" on chart paper
- assorted colored markers
- 24″ x 36″ lined newsprint and tag board chart paper
- pocket chart
- manila sentence strips

   To prepare for Carleen's visits, Sally immersed her kindergartners in reading nursery rhymes. She used big-book, small-book, and charted versions of these tales. For several weeks during daily shared reading, Sally returned to these rhymes for repeated readings, calling attention to the humor, the predictability of the language, and the stories the verses tell. The kindergartners chanted refrains and participated in dramatizations. Through the multiple rereadings, they were learning the story lines and becoming acquainted with the vocabulary from the rhymes. This would support their ability to create new verses during the shared writing retelling with Carleen.

   On the first day she visited, Carleen and the students decided to rewrite the familiar nursery rhyme "Little Miss Muffet." Carleen wrote the rhyme on sentence strips and placed them in a pocket chart. She invited students to point and read the rhyme several times. Then they began rewriting the poem. Here's a bit of the teacher-students exchange.

Use transparency film for copying rewritten nursery rhymes for students to read on an overhead projector placed on the floor. Place white paper on the wall as a screen. Keep each transparency safe in a zippered plastic bag.

◄ *Amy Dux's first graders enjoy reading their re-written nursery rhymes on the overhead projector.*

Photocopy the class versions of nursery rhymes, and have students illustrate them. Collate these into enough books for each student to have one to take home. Place extra copies of the book in the library corner for students to read and enjoy.

Mrs. Payne:	Since "Little Miss Muffet" is the rhyme we've decided to rewrite, let's think about how we might start.
Joanne:	I think we should put someone's name for Little Miss Muffet.
Mrs. Payne:	That might be a good way to begin. Whose name could we put?
Keith:	Erika's name, because it's her birthday.
Mrs. Payne:	We'll make that our birthday present to Erika. We'll put her name in the rhyme. Erika, would you like that? (Erika smiles and nods.) The first line starts, *Little Miss Muffet sat on a tuffett eating her curds and whey.* Where will I put Erika's name?
Ken:	As the first word.
Mrs. Payne:	Let's try that by saying the first line and trying *Erika* as the first word: *Erika Little Miss Muffet sat on a tuffett eating her curds and whey.*
Danielle:	No, that doesn't make sense. We need to put the word *Erika* where *Muffet* is because Muffet's her name.
Mrs. Payne:	Let's try Danielle's suggestion and see if it sounds right and makes sense. *Little Miss Erika sat on a tuffett eating her curds and whey.*
Tony:	Yes, it's in the right place. It makes sense.
Mrs. Payne:	Let's write *Erika* on this sentence strip. Who can help me spell *Erika*?
Jason:	It's on our word wall.
Sarah:	Ask Erika.
Mrs. Payne:	Those are two good ideas. We know that our names are on the word wall and we can ask Erika. Erika, can you write your name for us?
	(Erika writes her name in a different color than the text and places it in the pocket chart.)
Mrs. Payne:	Look at the next part, *sat on a tuffett.* Who wants to predict what a *tuffett* is?
	(Carleen engages students in a discussion of new vocabulary.)
Sammie:	It's a cushion.
Joi:	Maybe, a pillow.
Jeff:	A chair.
Mrs. Payne:	I think you're close, Jeff. It's a stool, a chair that is low to the ground. What word can we use for *tuffett?* Where could Little Miss Erika sit?
Paul:	On a sofa.
Ryan:	The ground.
Rose:	On a beanbag.
Students:	Yeah, a beanbag!
Mrs. Payne:	Where will I put the word *beanbag?*
Eileen:	Put it where *tuffett* is.

Mrs. Payne:	Let's try that. Read with me: *Little Miss Erika sat on a beanbag.* That makes sense and sounds okay. We need to write *beanbag.* Clap *beanbag.* How many parts do you hear?
Sarah:	Two.
Mrs. Payne:	Yes, Sarah, there's two parts in *beanbag.* Let's say the first part slowly—*b-eee(a)-nn.* What sound do you hear first?
John:	There's a *b.* I hear *bee,* like a buzzing bee.
Mrs. Payne:	John, can you write the letter *b?*
John:	Which way do I make a *b?*
Mrs. Payne:	I'm glad you're thinking about the way to make a *b.* I remember a *b* by thinking of the word *belly. Belly* starts with a *b.* Watch me as I make a *b.* Straight line down and a belly in front. Make a *b* with me. Make a *b* here for the word, *beanbag.*
	(Mrs. Payne and the kindergartners continue to engage in dialogue and complete a draft of the nursery rhyme verse.)

Little Miss Erika

Little Miss Erika sat on a beanbag
Eating her toast and syrup.
Along came a fly and sat in her syrup,
And scared Miss Erika away.

On the following day, Carleen displayed the sentence strips of the rewritten nursery rhyme, "Little Miss Erika." She and the students read their innovation of the verse several times and began recopying the verse as a chart for their read-around-the-room wall. Recopying the nursery rhyme provided Carleen with another opportunity to talk about capital letters for names and for words in a title. Her conversation went like this.

Quick Tip

Provide a flannelboard and felt pieces depicting nursery rhymes to encourage students to take part in retellings. Commercially prepared felt nursery rhymes are available (see Appendix).

◀ *Students enjoy retelling nursery rhymes on a flannelboard.*

Mrs. Payne:	Yesterday we wrote a new version of "Little Miss Muffet." Today we'll copy it, so it'll be part of our read-around-the-room charts. Let's start with the title, "Little Miss Erika." I'll put the title at the top. Titles are special. We'll need to use a capital letter for the first letter of each word. How many words are in our title?
John:	Three.
Mrs. Payne:	How many capital letters will I have?
Doris:	We need an L for *Little*.
Howard:	And an M for *Miss* and an E for *Erika*. Three.
Mrs. Payne:	Yes. We need three capital letters, one to start each word in our title. Who can write the capital letter for *Little*?
Jason:	I can.
	(Jason writes the capital letter for *Little*, while Carleen fills in the remaining letters.)
Mrs. Payne:	Let's write *Miss*. Maria, can you make the capital M, since your name starts with a capital M?
	(Maria writes a capital M, and Carleen fills in the remaining letters.)
Mrs. Payne:	What do we put next?
Erika:	My name.
Mrs. Payne:	Erika, come and write your name. Whenever we write a name, we always use a capital letter, because names are special. My name starts with a capital P for *Payne*. Jason's name starts with a capital J. Eileen's name starts with a capital E like Erika's.
	(Carleen continues to copy the text, thinking aloud about the use of capital letters for names and allowing kindergartners to write the parts they know. Later the chart with "Little Miss Erika" was added to a class book of nursery rhymes.)

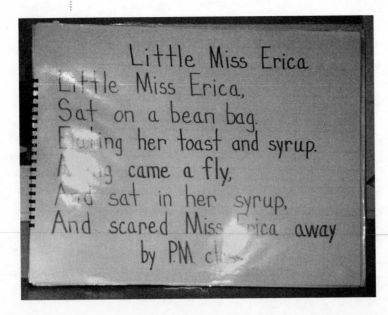

Sally Murray's kindergartners' version of "Little Miss Muffet" becomes "Little Miss Erika."

Using Wordless Books
With First Graders

Speech is the first communication skill children acquire. We use wordless books to involve our students in "story talk." Wordless books help students look carefully at the illustrations to derive meaning or to unlock a familiar word—both important reading strategies for emergent readers. For our shared writing experiences, we carefully select wordless books with the following characteristics.

* Texts that represent common student experiences or familiar stories. Literature selections might include *Deep in the Forest, New Baby,* or *Sunshine.*

* Narrative texts that have a predictable or repetitive story structure which permits easy reading. *Mouse Around, A Boy, a Dog, and a Frog,* and *Do You Want to be My Friend?* are three of many good choices.

* Texts with clear illustrations that are rich with color and support the story line. Favorites include *Good Night Gorilla, Little Red Riding Hood,* and *Good Dog, Carl.*

Here is an effective way to use wordless books. Mary spent four sessions doing this activity with Terry Creamer's first graders. You'll need:

* wordless book *Deep in the Forest* by Brinton Turkle (Big Book version, if possible)
* copy of Byron Barton's *The Three Bears*
* Stick On™ removable sentence strips, approximately 2″x 8″ (see DLM resources in Appendix)
* assorted markers
* chart paper

Mary assembled a collection of wordless books and immersed the students in them for several weeks. After enjoying the stories and retelling them by looking at the illustrations, the students were ready for a shared writing activity to compose the text for *Deep in the Forest,* Brinton Turkle's wordless turnabout version of *The Three Bears* in which little bear visits the home of Goldilocks.

Guidelines for Reading Wordless Books With Students

- Take picture walks through wordless books, and demonstrate how you are able to read the story by looking at the illustrations.
- Use rich, descriptive story language with your retelling.
- Add your own details to story lines, but remain within the parameters of the story.
- Invent story character names, and speak as some of the characters.
- Create sound effects to tell the story.
- Engage students in the readings of the texts with you, or pair students to do retellings.

For several days before Mary's visit, Terry read Byron Barton's version of *The Three Bears* during the daily shared reading time. The students needed to know the original story in order to create a text for *Deep in the Forest*.

On the first day, Mary began by taking a picture walk through *Deep in the Forest*, telling the story through the pictures. She invited the first graders to notice that this story was similar to another they had heard.

Mrs. Schulman:	Does this book remind you of another story?
Pamela:	It's like *The Three Bears*, but it's the little bear that makes a mess instead of Goldilocks.
Mrs. Schulman:	That's right, Pamela. Does anyone remember what happened in that story?
Michael:	Yes. Papa Bear's porridge was too hot. Mama Bear's porridge was too cold, but Baby Bear's porridge was just right!
	(Students continue to share story events and phrases from the story.)
Mrs. Schulman:	You've remembered so many of the story events and words from *The Three Bears*. Thinking about what happened in *The Three Bears* and remembering some of the words from that story will help us tell this story. Listen as I read the pictures in this story.
	(Mary reads the illustrations of *Deep in the Forest* using rich, descriptive story language. She and the first graders discuss the similarities and differences in the two stories.)

Later in the day, Mary and the first graders reread *Deep in the Forest*. She invited students to participate in an oral retelling by letting them dramatize parts of the story while she read. She set out the flannelboard with *The Three Bears* felt pieces and suggested that students retell the story during literacy center time.

On the next day, Mary returned to *Deep in the Forest* and reread the picture story. She wanted the first graders to be well-acquainted with the story plot and language. Mary and the students began to write their text by making a list of events from the story. Here's a bit of how she got started.

Quick Tip

Have students tape record their written retelling of their wordless story. Put the students' tape in the listening center with a copy of the book.

Mrs. Schulman: Today we'll get ready to write the words for our story, *Deep in the Forest*. To help us remember what happened in the story, we'll make a list of ideas. Think about the order that the story happened. What came first? Next? After that?

(Mary records the student ideas on chart paper. If you think your students need extra support for reading the list of ideas, include pictures.)

Here's the chart Mary and the first graders made to record story events.

Deep in the Forest Sequence Chart

Beginning:
- Little Bear runs away from his family.
- Little Bear finds the door to a house open and goes in.

Middle:
- He saw three bowls of cereal. He ate the baby's cereal.
- He saw three chairs. He broke the baby's chair.
- He went to the bedroom.
- He jumped on the bed and made a mess.
- He heard a noise and hid under the bed covers.
- Goldilocks and her family return and find a mess in their house
- Someone has eaten their cereal.
- Someone has sat in their chairs.
- Someone has messed their bedroom.

Ending:
- Little Bear wakes up and sees Goldilocks and her family.
- Goldilocks and her family chase Little Bear away.
- Little Bear runs back to his family.

On the following day, Mary displayed the copy of *Deep in the Forest* and read the list of story ideas and events the first graders had generated on the previous day.

Mrs. Schulman: Today we'll take our list of story ideas and use them to write the words for our story, *Deep in the Forest*. I'll put our words on these Special Stick On™ notes (see DLM in the Appendix). Then, we'll place them on the correct pages in our book. Our first idea says *Little Bear runs away from his family*. Since this is a folk tale, how might we begin?

Bob: *Once upon a time, a bear ran away from his family.*

Mrs. Schulman: Is there another way we might start?

Donna: *Little Bear was unhappy. He decided to leave his family.*

Mrs. Schulman: Both of those ideas are good ways to begin. Who would like to start with *Once upon a time*? Who would like to start with *Little Bear was unhappy*? Okay, we'll start with *Once upon a time*. I'll write it on our Stick On™ note. Where will I put it? At the top or bottom of the page?

(Mary continues to negotiate the wording and placement of the text with students.)

Mary assists first graders as they write the words for the story Deep in the Forest.

After Mary and the first graders completed writing the retelling of *Deep in the Forest*, Terry and her students reread the book during the daily shared readings time and subsequently placed it in the class library.

Using Predictable Stories With Second Graders

Predictable books—with stories characterized by a repetitive story line, a logical sequence of events, and frequent repetition of sentence patterns—help beginning readers and writers acquire important literacy skills. The rhythm, rhyme, and repetition of these stories invite students to actively participate in the reading and to make meaning because they can anticipate the text. Also, since many of the words are repeated frequently, predictable books support the development of a sight vocabulary.

In some predictable books, such as *I Know an Old Lady*, the story events and language are cumulative; in others, such as Stan and Jan Berenstain's *Bears in the Night*, the stories are circular, beginning and ending with the same setting, event, or problem. Some predictable books include a familiar sequence such as numbers or days of the week as found in Eric Carle's *The Very Hungry Caterpillar*.

Choose predictable books that offer familiar concepts, supportive illustrations, and natural language patterns to engage your students in a meaningful shared writing experience.

Here's how Carleen and a group of Jacqueline Fee's second graders wrote a retelling of a predictable text with a circular story pattern. Try it with your students.

You'll need:

❖ copy of *Millions of Cats* by Wanda Gag
❖ chart paper and newsprint
❖ assorted markers
❖ construction paper

Tip Box

Favorite Circular Stories

● *Bears in the Night*

● *Buzz, Buzz, Buzz*

● *If You Give a Mouse a Cookie*

● *If You Give a Moose a Muffin*

● *If You Give a Pig a Pancake*

● *The Old Woman Who Lived in a Vinegar Bottle*

Quick Tip

Dramatize rewritten predictable stories. Children find it easy to memorize their lines because of the repetitive nature of the tales. Design backdrops for the story settings and make simple puppets and props. Store the materials for each drama in a box with a copy of the text.

Carleen gathered a collection of circle stories for Jacqueline to read during shared reading time. Jacqueline began by introducing *Bears in the Night* as a circle story and on succeeding days reread it as an "old favorite." Students enjoyed the humor of the story line repeating itself. As Jacqueline continued reading circle stories, her second graders began to recognize the circular pattern in these tales—they began and ended with the same setting, event, or problem. This background information would help them retell *Millions of Cats* in a shared writing with Carleen.

On the first day, Carleen brought a big book version of *Millions of Cats* for a shared reading. She asked the students to listen carefully to the story so they could do a retelling of it later. She began by asking the second graders what they knew about a retelling.

Mrs. Payne:	Can anyone tell me what a *retelling* is?
Ellen:	It's when you repeat a story.
Stacey:	It's when you tell a story again.
Mrs. Payne:	Yes. A retelling is to repeat or tell a story again. We'll do a written retelling of the story *Millions of Cats* by writing it again in our own words. We'll need to remember what happened in the story. *Millions of Cats* is a circle story. Think about a circle. What do you know about a circle?
Donna:	It's round.
Michael:	It has no points.
Zaim:	It goes on and on.
Mrs. Payne:	You're all right! You're using what you know about shapes. As I read, think of how your ideas about circles fit into this story. Think about why we might call *Millions of Cats* a circle story.
	(Carleen reads *Millions of Cats*, and in a discussion afterwards, helps the children discover its circular pattern.)
Mrs. Payne:	Think about how our story began. Think about how it ended. What happened in between?
Dolores:	The old man and old woman wanted a cat.
Bill:	They found hundreds, and thousands, and millions, and billions, and trillions of cats, but they ended up with only one cat!
Mrs. Payne:	Can you see a circle pattern?
Jose:	Yes, because they wanted one cat, and they ended up with only one cat. But lots happened before they got that one cat.
Mrs. Payne:	Our story starts and ends with the same event, having one cat. It's like a circle. If you start in one place on the circle and go around, you'll come back to the same spot. Did anyone notice another circle pattern in the story? Think about something that was the same at the beginning and end.
Amy:	It began at the old lady's and old man's house and ended at their house.
	(Carleen and the second graders continue to discuss story events.)

Next, Carleen retold the story by "reading" the illustrations, inviting students to participate in the refrain, *hundreds, and thousands, and millions, and billions, and trillions of cats.* She left *Millions of Cats* out on the easel and suggested that students do an oral retelling during their literacy center time.

On the second day, Carleen reread *Millions of Cats*. Then, as she recalled story details with the students, she recorded them on a circle chart. The chart would help students plan for the written retelling of *Millions of Cats*.

Mrs. Payne:	We'll need to get ready for our retelling of *Millions of Cats*. I've made a circle. Think of it as a pie, and each piece of the pie is an idea from the story. We'll use this circle chart to help us write our retelling. We'll start at the top of the circle or pie. Think about how the story began.
Cindy:	The old man and old woman were lonely. They wanted a cat.
Mrs. Payne:	I'll write that idea at the top of our chart. What happened next?
Amy:	The old man went looking for a cat and found one, two, three...
Students:	Hundreds, and thousands, and millions, and billions and trillions of cats.
Mrs. Payne:	I'll put that in the next piece of our pie chart.
	(Carleen continues to write the story events until they are all recorded in a circular fashion on the chart.)

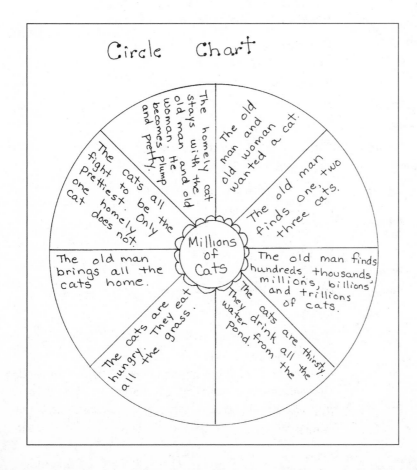

Circle Chart

Millions of Cats

The old man and old woman wanted a cat.

The old man finds one, two, three cats.

The old man finds hundreds, thousands, millions, billions, and trillions of cats.

They drink all the water from the pond. The cats are thirsty.

The cats are hungry. They eat all the grass.

The old man brings all the cats home.

The cats all fight to be the prettiest. Only one homely cat does not.

The homely cat stays with the old man and old woman. He becomes plump and pretty.

On the following day, Carleen brought large sheets of newsprint, on which she and the students would write the retelling of *Millions of Cats*.

Mrs. Payne:	Today we'll look at our circle chart of story ideas and use it to write a retelling of our story, *Millions of Cats*. How can we start?
Shirley:	Once upon a time there was an old man and old woman.
Tommy:	An old man and old woman wanted a cat.
Sam:	Once there was an old man and an old woman.
Mrs. Payne:	All of those ideas are good ones. Since this is a make-believe story, *Once upon a time* might be a good way to begin. I'll write that in. Look at our chart and read with me. (Students read.) What happened next?
Don:	They were lonely and wanted a cat.
David:	The old woman wanted a cat so the old man went to get one.
Mrs. Payne:	Which of those ideas gives us more information for our story?
	(Carleen and the second graders continue to compose the story together, referring to the circle chart for ideas. Carleen acts as the scribe, writing the story on newsprint. When they come to the repetitive phrase, students write portions of the text.)
Mrs. Payne:	I want you to help me write the repeating part of the story— hundreds and thousands, and millions, and billions, and trillions of cats. Let's start by clapping for the word *hundreds*. How many parts do you hear?
Josh:	Two.
Mrs. Payne:	Say the first part slowly.
Students:	H-UU-NN.
Mrs. Payne:	What letters should I put for the first part?
Joanne:	H-u-m.
Mrs. Payne:	Almost. The first part *Hun* is like *fun*.
Joanne:	H-u-n. It's an *n*.
Mrs. Payne:	Come and write the first part, *Hun*.
	(Joanne writes *Hun*.)
Mrs. Payne:	Clap *hundred* again. We wrote the first part. Say the second part slowly.
Students:	D-RR-EE-D.
Mrs. Payne:	Rachel, what letters will we write for the last part?
Rachel:	r-e-d.
Mrs. Payne:	You're close. It's hard to hear the sounds in *dred*. There's a *d* in front of the *r*.
	(Carleen continues to engage the students in the writing of the dialogue for the refrain. When writing the words *millions, and billions, and trillions,* she points out that the same sounds and letters are used at the end of these words. She

shows them how, if they knew *millions*, they could get *billions* and *trillions*. The refrain appears several times in the text, but Carleen shares the writing of the refrain with the children only the first time, copying it into the text herself thereafter.)

Students from Jacqueline Fee's second grade created a retelling of Millions of Cats. ▶

On the last day, Carleen and the second graders took their newsprint story and sectioned it into pages for a wall frieze. She copied the text on white paper and glued it to construction paper cut in the shape of cats. Students completed the illustrations. Later the class version of *Millions of Cats* was placed on a wall outside the classroom.

Second graders' wall frieze of Millions of Cats

Quick Tip

With your students, use a computer to write rebus stories for predictable books. Replace some of the words, usually nouns, with pictures. Print individual student copies and place some copies in a browsing box for students to read and enjoy during independent reading time.

Students in Sarah Cobb's kindergarten class created a rebus retelling of the circle story The Best Nest.

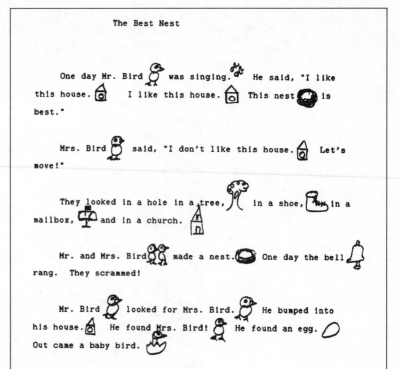

In this chapter we've described ways to create innovations and written retellings for nursery rhymes, wordless books, and predictable stories. In these shared writing experiences, we look for ways to share the pen with our students by composing and writing together. The literature we read to our students models story structure and provides support for their own writing.

CHAPTER 5

Shared Writing in the Content Areas

"Children learn to write by reading and writing many different kinds of text."

—New Zealand Ministry of Education, _Dancing With the Pen_

I t's after lunch, and Suzanne Comer has gathered her 25 first graders around her so that she can begin reading aloud the nonfiction book _Squirrels All Year Long_. Her students will be studying squirrels as part of their science curriculum, and she plans to include informational writing in the unit. Suzanne regularly reads informational material to her students, because she recognizes that it's another good way to demonstrate how written language works. It's also a way to help her students learn the language and conventions of informational writing. Suzanne's first graders frequently create informational webs, construct diagrams, and keep a class learning log as part of their shared writing experiences in first grade.

Above: Suzanne Comer's first graders created an informational web about squirrels.

Suzanne and her colleagues at Centre Ridge and Halley continually search for better ways to integrate language arts into the content areas. Most students at the primary level have little experience with informational writing. Realizing this, our teachers make every effort to explore, demonstrate, and engage young writers in *writing to learn*. Shared writing experiences in the content areas give our teachers plenty of chances to model concepts about print, the conventions of language, and how writers think, plan, and compose.

Developing Informational Webs With Kindergartners

Informational webs help primary students organize and record the information they're studying. Through shared writing experiences, teachers can demonstrate how to classify facts and show students that writers use different techniques to plan their writing. The web also serves as a written classroom resource for a unit of study. Sometimes teachers add illustrations to a web to provide support for the students in recalling and reading information. Here's how Carleen worked with Helene Stapleton and her kindergartners to develop an informational web on birds.

Carleen and Helene began by going to the school library and gathering books about birds. Since their goal was to expose students to such characteristics of nonfiction as an index, a table of contents, and captions, they included books with these features.

Carleen and the children would construct the web as the students learned new facts. Asking questions about what the students already knew about birds would help focus the web. So to prepare for Carleen's visit, Helene and the kindergartners talked and shared writing ideas on two charts labeled *What Do We Think We Know About Birds* and *What Do We Want to Know About Birds*. There were no right or wrong answers; all the information the students gave was accepted. It would be verified as the students learned new facts. This approach helps students understand that writers revisit their writing to clarify, change, or add new ideas.

What We Think We Know About Birds	What Do We Want to Know About Birds
Birds use twigs to build nests.	Do birds sleep?
They lay eggs.	Do birds have teeth?
They eat worms.	How do birds fly?
Birds fly south.	Why do birds take baths?
Robins are a kind of bird.	How many babies do they have?
Hummingbirds are really tiny.	Where do birds live?

After the students completed the charts, Helene asked, "Did you notice a special mark I used over and over again at the end of each line on this list?" As she asked this, she pointed to questions under "What We Want to Know About Birds." This was the perfect opportunity to link to a previous discussion on using question marks.

Using the student charts, Helene and Carleen determined the categories for focus on the web. They cut a large piece of seamless paper (36" x 54") and labeled it as follows:

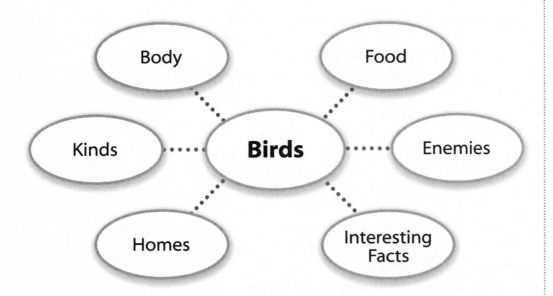

The following day, Carleen visited Helene's classroom and introduced the web.

Mrs. Payne:	Yesterday you made a list with Mrs. Stapleton of some of the things you think you know about birds and then you made a list of other questions you have about birds. Mrs. Stapleton and I took your ideas and wrote them down so we can make connections about what we're learning about birds. When we connect the ideas, it'll be like a spider's web. Think about how the spider makes a web. It goes in different directions. When we put our bird ideas and facts on this web, we'll call it an *informational web*. Say that with me.
	(Students and teachers repeat the words *informational web*.)
Mrs. Payne:	Now let's look at the informational web Mrs. Stapleton and I started about birds on this large paper. We'll put the facts we learn about birds on different parts of our web. If we get information about what birds eat, we will put it under *food*. If we learn something about birds' houses, we'll put it under *homes*.
	(Carleen continues to explain the categories of the web.)

Carleen read aloud Cathryn Sill's book *About Birds*, reminding students to listen for information they could add to the class web. Afterwards, the discussion went like this:

Mrs. Payne:	As you were listening to *About Birds*, who heard an idea or fact we can put on our informational web?
Sarah:	It said some birds build their nests on the ground.
Mrs. Payne:	That was interesting, wasn't it, Sarah? I'm not sure that's a very safe place to put a nest. Where on the web should we put that idea?
Sarah:	I think it talks about where their home is.
Mrs. Payne:	Right! It belongs under *Homes*. I'll put a dot to show us that this is the first idea. For our web, we can use *shortcut* writing. I'll write our ideas a short way. I can say *in the ground*. Our idea is under *Homes*, so we'll know that it means *bird homes can be in the ground*. Was there another bit of information we can add to our web?
Eileen:	Birds have feathers.
Mrs. Payne:	Where does your idea belong?
Eileen:	Under *Interesting Facts*.

Mrs. Payne:	It *is* an interesting fact. But is there a better place on our web for this idea?
Tom:	Under *Body*.
Mrs. Payne:	What helped you decide that, Tom?
Tom:	Because feathers are on the bird's body.
Mrs. Payne:	Yes. *Body* is a better place to put that information. Sometimes we have to decide where our information will fit the best. I'll write *feathers* under *Body*. Any other facts about birds?
Pat:	Birds sing.
Mrs. Payne:	Where could we put that?
Pat:	I think that could go under *Interesting Facts*.
Mrs. Payne:	Could we put that information in any other place on our web? Let's check.
	(Mrs. Payne and the students check all the categories and determine that Pat's idea should go under *Interesting Facts*. The kindergartners continue to suggest information.)
Mrs. Payne:	We've added some new information to our bird web. I think it would help us remember our ideas if we drew a picture to go with each idea. I have small squares of paper, so we can draw pictures to match our ideas. Who would like to show us a bird's home in the ground? Jason, how might we do that?
Jason:	You could put leaves on the ground and show a nest in the leaves.
Mrs. Payne:	That seems like a good way to show us birds build their nests in the ground. When you've finished your drawing, give it to me and I'll tape it to our chart.

Carleen shared informational books about birds for several days. She and the kindergartners continued to add illustrations and new details. Before adding to the web each day, they reviewed the information on it. The informational web was displayed in the classroom so that Helene and her students could refer to it as a summary of their learning. Some students took information from the web and wrote about birds in their journals. Here's how the web looked after several days of reading.

Body

- feathers
- wings
- beak or bill
- different colors

Food

- berries
- seeds
- insects
- worms

Kinds

- robin
- hummingbird
- owls
- peacock
- penguin
- flamingo

Birds

Enemies

- environment
- cats
- snakes
- cars
- other birds

Homes

- ground
- straw
- tall buildings
- grass
- trees
- bird box

Interesting Facts

- Penguins can't fly.
- Male birds are more colorful.
- Hummingbird is smallest bird.
- Birds hatch from an egg.
- Birds have an egg tooth.

Recording in Learning Logs or Journals With First Graders

Keeping a learning log or journal helps students think about their learning by writing about it. Writing in their journals they observe, predict, list, draw, label, chart, web, brainstorm, and ask questions. For Centre Ridge and Halley teachers, learning logs provide opportunities to demonstrate strategies that enable students to write to learn. And by reviewing students' journals, our teachers can evaluate their teaching. They can see what students know and use the information to adjust lessons appropriately when necessary.

A *class learning log* is one of the ways Halley and Centre Ridge teachers introduce primary students to the various formats for informational writing. For a class learning log, consider recording information you've observed or learned through talking, listening, reading, hands-on activities, audio-visual materials, field trips, or interviews. When Cathy Yerington and her first graders were beginning a science unit on seeds, Mary used shared writing sessions to demonstrate how to keep a class learning log. She recorded in the log the class' steps of a lima bean experiment, as well as students' observations, predictions, and learning.

Before working with Cathy's class, Mary made the class learning log by stapling together 15 sheets of 18″ x 24″ newsprint (you could use oak tag for a sturdier log). In the classroom, she set the stage for the experiment by explaining to the first graders what they'd be doing.

Mrs. Schulman: You've been talking about all kinds of seeds the past few days. Today, you and your partner are going to take a close look at a lima bean seed. You should use your magnifying lens to look at it closely. Think about how it looks, feels, and smells. Then we'll meet to talk about everything you've noticed or observed.

(In pairs, students talk about their observations of a lima bean seed.)

Next, Mary gathered students in an open area on the rug and placed the class learning log on an easel so the students could see her write. She began by explaining to the first graders how they would use the log.

Mrs. Schulman: Our class learning log is a place to record what we've observed and what we're learning. We will add information every day. First, let's think of a title for our log. I'll record suggestions on the chalkboard. Who has an idea?

Taylor: Our Learning Log.

Brad: Experiments With Seeds.

Joey: Lima Beans.

Amy: Lima Bean Experiment.

(Mrs. Schulman and the first graders decide on *The Lima Bean Experiment* for their title, and Mrs. Schulman writes it on the cover. Inside, on the first page, she writes *Day 1*.)

Mrs. Schulman: Each day we'll begin our log by writing the date and the day of our experiment. Think about what you did with your partner today. How can we write that in the learning log?

Richard: *We looked at our lima bean seed with a partner.*

Donna: *We met with our partner to look at a lima bean.*

Mrs. Schulman: Okay, we have two different ways we can write what you did. They both mean the same thing, so we'll have to decide which way we like better.

(Mrs. Schulman negotiates with the students to decide what to write. As they continue to share their observations about the lima bean seeds, she writes them on the DAY 1 page, rereading the entry with the students.)

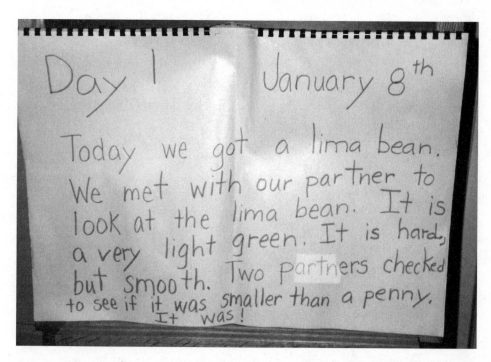

This is the entry Cathy Yerington's first graders wrote in their learning log on the first day.

On the following day, Mary and Cathy meet with the first graders briefly to reread the previous day's entry. Mary explains the next steps in the experiment:

Mrs. Schulman: Today, you'll need three things. First, a wet paper towel; second, a lima bean from the soaking dish; and third, a resealable bag. You'll use these to make a *growing chamber* for the lima bean.

(Mary demonstrates how to make the growing chamber. Then Cathy and Mary help the students as they prepare their own growing chamber. When the class is finished, they gather on the rug again.)

Mrs. Schulman: Now, we'll need to record what we did today. Do you remember how to start each new entry in a learning log?

Jason: We should put the date and *Day 2* at the top.

Mrs. Schulman: That's right. If we want to go back and check to see what day we did something or observed something, the date will help us.

(Mary labels the next page DAY 2 and writes the date.)

Mrs. Schulman: Think about what we did first. Then what next? And then what? What we did will help other people know what to do if they want to try the same experiment.

(Mary records the following student responses in the log.)

Day 2 - January 9th

1. We got a paper towel and wet it.

2. We folded the paper towel two times.

3. We put a soaked lima bean inside the folded paper towel.

4. We put it inside a plastic bag and closed it. We call it the growing chamber.

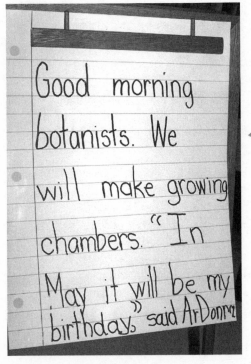

◄ *First grade teacher Terry Creamer connected her morning message to her class science unit on seeds.*

On *Day 3* when Mary and the students observed their lima beans, they decided that since nothing had happened, they would predict what they thought would happen next. Mary accepted and recorded all student predictions, knowing that they would return to that page in the log later to check which predictions actually occurred. During the next few days, Mary and the students continued to observe the lima bean in the growing chamber, recorded observations, and made new predictions. Some entries were brief, because the students weren't able to observe any changes from the previous entry.

Mrs. Schulman: *Has anyone noticed anything happening to their lima bean? (Many students said no.) What will we write so we'll know that?*

Carol: *Nothing is happening.*

Annie: *The lima bean looks the same as it did yesterday.*

Mrs. Schulman: *Okay, let's begin by writing DAY 5 at the top and the date. Then we can write what you said. Who can write Day 5?*

The fact that the first graders weren't noticing any changes at one point prompted a discussion. The first graders wondered: *What will happen if a lima bean doesn't grow?* Mary suggested that they put the question in the class learning log and together think of some answers to the question. Here's what they came up with.

What Will Happen if the Lima Bean Doesn't Grow?

- We'll have to start again.

- We'll have to try another experiment.

- We'll have to use another kind of seed.

- We can try putting it in the window.

Mary and Cathy believe the class learning log played a significant role in the success of the lesson. The first graders observed, predicted and recorded what they were learning. The shared writing demonstrations and co-construction of the log entries helped them connect new strands of learning to what they already knew about seeds and how plants grow. Shared writing in the class learning log gave them the opportunity to do informational writing.

Using Diagrams With Second Graders

Think of a diagram as a graphic text that can show, list, or measure the parts of a whole for students. In diagrams, the words and pictures work together to make the meaning that students will read and interpret. Primary students who are not yet fluent writers may find it easier to communicate information visually rather than exclusively in words. Here is one way Mary helped second graders learn about making a diagram.

The second graders in Molly Connolly's classroom had been studying crickets. After reading about crickets and observing their own crickets in a group-created habitat, Mary and the second graders labeled an enlarged poster of a cricket drawn by one of the students.

Students began by brainstorming what they knew about the parts of a cricket. Mary listed all the parts of the cricket on chart paper as the students generated the list. Here is a snapshot of how the session unfolded.

Mrs. Schulman:	We've been reading about crickets and observing them each day now for a week. Let's think about what we know about the cricket's parts. We'll list the parts on chart paper. What could we title this list?
Laurie:	*The Cricket's Parts.*
Mrs. Schulman:	You thought about starting with what this list will be about. Any other way we might write a title for the list?
Charles:	*All About Crickets.*
	(After thinking of another possible title, Mary and the students settle on *The Cricket's Parts.* She writes the title at the top of the page.)
Mrs. Schulman:	What part of the cricket should I write down first?
Paul:	Abdomen.
Mrs. Schulman:	What parts do you hear in that word?
Paul:	Ab-do-men. It has three parts.
Mrs. Schulman:	Do you know a word that starts like the first part?
Abigail:	Yes, my name.
Mrs. Schulman:	What do I put first, Abigail?
Abigail:	/ab/—A-b.
Mrs. Schulman:	What's the second part? How will I write the next part?
Carlos:	D-o.
Mrs. Schulman:	The last part?
Peter:	M-e-n.
Mrs. Schulman:	What else can we list as a part?
Robin:	Head.
Mrs. Schulman:	Robin, show us where to write the word *head* on the list.
	(Robin points to the space under the word *abdomen*.)

Mrs. Schulman:	That's right. When we write a list, we write each new idea below the idea we just wrote. The words go down the page on a list. What would we do if the list came down to the end of the page?
Jan:	Start another row or list.
Mrs. Schulman:	Yes. We could start a new column. What else could we do?
Sam:	Start a new list on another paper.

abdomen	6 legs
head	ovipositor
palpi or mouth part	4 wings
thorax	2 antennae
compound eyes	

On the following day, Mary and the students reread the brainstormed list of cricket's parts. She cut apart the list of words on the chart and distributed each word to the students. She asked each student to find the part on the diagram and place the label near it. Mary and the students drew arrows and lines to connect labels to the picture part. To encourage students to notice how much graphic information was included in the diagram of the cricket, Mary and the students played Cricket Quizmo.

Mrs. Schulman:	Remember when we played Animal Quizmo? A person asked a question, and the person who answered it asked the next question. So before we begin, let's take a minute to look at the diagram and think of a question you could ask.
Peggy:	How many legs are on each side?
Dion:	I counted three.
Dion:	Where is the cricket's ovipositor?
Tammy:	It's at the back.
Tammy:	Who can name the body parts of the cricket?
	(Mary and the second graders continue to use the diagram to create and answer questions.)

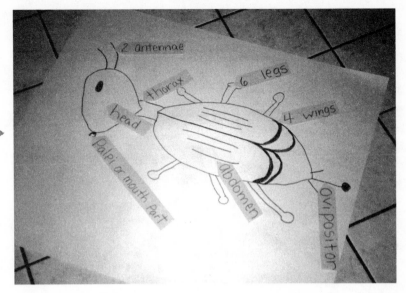

Students used this cricket diagram to play Cricket Quizmo. ▶

Later Mary and the students wrote the questions on sentence strips and placed the sentence strips in a pocket next to the display of the poster. During literacy center time, the second graders referred to the diagram to answer the questions when "reading the room."

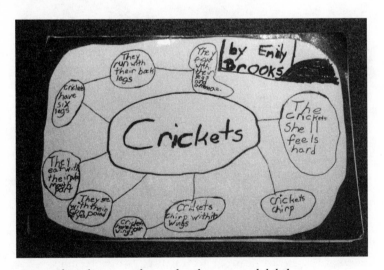

A second grader wrote this cricket diagram with labels.

Quick Tip

Try having students write diagrams independently if you think they're ready. After you and they have created a diagram on a poster together, remove the word labels from the original poster and put magnetic strips on the backs. Put these on the chalkboard for students to use as a reference. Then give them blank pieces of paper and ask them to use the visual of the original poster and the list of labels as a reference to write their own diagrams.

*B*ecause many informational texts use visual elements to communicate information, students need opportunities to write and read such visual texts as diagrams, maps, graphs, and tables. Using diagrams and labels helps students learn how visual texts work; how pictures, symbols, and words together make meaning. Using shared writing in the content areas is a practical way to integrate writing and the curriculum with young students.

A Home-School Connection for Shared Writing

"If people who are important to a child do not demonstrate that literacy is important, then why should a child believe that becoming literate is of any significance?"

–Nigel Hall and Anne Robinson, Looking at Literacy

Above: Sharon Williams writes with her son Xavier when she visits his first grade classroom.

We recognize that parents are the first teachers of the child and that the home environment can foster and nurture positive feelings toward literacy. By meeting and talking with parents, we can share some of the practical ways parents can participate in their children's learning. We help them understand that there are many occasions for shared writing in the home and that it is through shared writing that students can learn to become independent writers. We point out that these shared writing experiences are informal opportunities to illustrate writing as a natural part of everyday life.

At Centre Ridge and Halley, we welcome help from our students' parents. In this chapter we'll discuss how we inform parents about their children's language development and how we encourage parents to practice shared writing with their child at home.

Language Is Developmental

We usually begin by reminding parents how children develop language. We ask them to think about how most children learn to talk in a relatively unconscious, functional way before they enter school. They move from babbling as a baby to speaking and interacting with others to have their needs met, to explore, to question, to express attitudes, and to share ideas and thoughts. Parents don't sit down with a set of rules or lessons to help their child learn to talk, but rather are involved in using language for real purposes and reasons in their daily lives. Just as children learn to talk by talking, they learn to write by writing.

We provide parents with a chart that shows the different stages of writing. We gather samples of writing that are representative of students in kindergarten, first grade, or second grade, and create a chart similar to the kindergarten sample chart shown here. It reminds parents about the developmental nature of writing and enables them to see where their child is on the writing continuum. We share the chart with parents at Back-to-School Night or during Parent-Teacher conference times.

Sample of kindergarten writing chart shared with Centre Ridge parents. ▶

Jennifer Hogue and her dad write a story during Centre Ridge's Family Language Arts Night.

Parental Support Is Important!

We show parents how to provide a supportive atmosphere for writing in the home. Our parents frequently expect their children to have adult competencies in writing and want them to write perfectly from the start. They ask us if they should spell words or be concerned if their child makes letters backwards or shows little interest in writing beyond scribbling. We've found that giving parents a list of practical suggestions helps them understand young writers, and encourages them to use shared writing opportunities at home. Here's a sample list:.

Writing With Your Child

❋ **Accept whatever the child writes: drawings, written attempts, approximate spellings.**

Mom: I like the way you put a *b* for baby.

Dad: You have most of the letters in *daddy*.

Mom: You put an *s* for *Sam*. Let's check to see if it is going the right way.

❋ **Believe—as the children do—that they can write.**

Dad: Let's leave a note for Mom telling her to get some pizza for dinner.

Don: I don't know how to write.

Dad: You know how to write your name, don't you?

Don: Yes.

Dad: Then, you can write your name when we sign the note.

❋ **Sit side by side so you can share in the writing experience.**

Mom: Pull up a chair next to me, so we can see what each other is writing.

❋ **Help children to explore their ideas and discover what they want to say by talking through their ideas with them.**

Mom: Grandma Lyn is sick. Let's make a card for her. What can we say?

Deirdre: We miss her. We want her to get better.

Mom: Yes, we could. Perhaps, we can even tell her we will come for a visit.

Deirdre: Can we tell her when we'll come?

Mom: Good idea. I'm glad we talked about what to say. Now we're ready to make Grandma Lyn's card.

❋ **Share in the writing when it becomes difficult or tricky for your child.**

Dad: I can write Grandpa's name in the letter. Names are sometimes hard to write.

❋ **Be willing to help a child say the word slowly and listen for the sounds of the letters, rather than just spelling the word.**

Mom: Say the word slowly. What do you hear first? What do you hear next? What do you hear last?

❋ **Focus on and celebrate what the child can do as a writer.**

Dad: I like how you tried to write the word *like* by yourself. Let me show you how close you are.

Back-to-School night is an opportune time to discuss, and encourage, shared writing at home. At Centre Ridge and Halley, our Back-to-School nights are early in the school year, so we have a captive audience! In our conversations with parents, we help inform them about the developmental stages of writing and emphasize the real contribution they can make to their own child's writing skills.

Yes, We Do Teach Phonics!

Back-to-School night is also the perfect time to clear up any possible misunderstandings such as, "Why don't you teach phonics?" Parents need to know that we *do* teach phonics; what's changed is how we teach it! We explain that real reading and real writing instruction have replaced isolated phonics worksheets in most classrooms and that beginning writers need to be able to listen for and hear sounds in words that they want to use in their writing.

We suggest to parents that when they write with their children, they use one of the techniques we use in the classroom: to have children say the word they need to spell *slowly* so they can learn how to hear and record sounds (see Chapter 1).

Mrs. Payne: *Best. Say that word slowly. Stretch it out. B-EEE-SSS-T. What do you hear first? What do you hear next? What else do you hear? What do you hear last?*

Parents' Writing Workshop

Another opportunity to let parents know some ways to support their children's writing is through a Parents' Writing Workshop. We invite parents to come for a morning or evening meeting to learn about writing. We try to create a relaxed atmosphere by serving refreshments and encouraging informal discussion. Here are some guidelines we've developed at Centre Ridge and Halley parent workshops.

❉ Begin by having parents recall their own school experiences with writing. You might be surprised to hear, "I had to write stories with at least 300 words," or "Every year we wrote about our summer vacation," or "My teacher used a red pencil all over my writing."

❉ Talk about why we write and how most of the writing we do serves a purpose, such as letters, messages, or lists. We like to start with the question, "What did you write today?"

❉ Show what writing looks like in your classroom by sharing examples from former students. We engage parents in a discussion about what the student writers have learned to do and let them know that approximate spelling has

Quick Tip

Collect and save representative student writing samples. Use these in workshops with parents and in focus lessons with your students.

a place in writing development. Parents will come away knowing about the stages of writing through which children need to progress.

✿ Demonstrate, with a group of students if possible, the process you use to teach writing. You might show how you choose a topic, how you plan for your writing with a drawing or by making a list, or how you reread your writing while composing to check if it makes sense. As parents see how you teach writing, they will learn some techniques to support their child's writing at home.

Opportunities for Shared Writing at Home

Provide parents with some specific suggestions for shared writing at home. Here are a few of our favorite ideas.

Making a Writer's Box or Drawer

Assemble a box or drawer of writing materials to help your child see that we write with many varied and interesting tools and that writing can be fun. Use a kitchen drawer, a shoe box, a tackle box, a plastic container or a child-size suitcase to hold the writing materials.

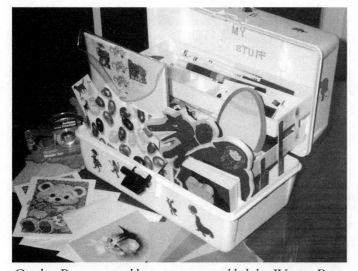

Candice Browning and her parents assembled this Writing Box to use at home.

Quick Tip

If you can't demonstrate the writing process at a parent workshop with actual students, consider creating a video tape. Make the tape available to parents for home viewing.

Quick Tip

Suggest to parents that they stimulate interest in writing by planning a special shopping trip with their child to look for interesting writing materials—pens, magic markers, colored pencils, neon crayons, colored chalk, "puffy" paint pens, and pencils. A variety of writing paper might include children's stationery, paper of various sizes and colors, and note pads. Also suggest that parents look for opportunities to get unused or discarded paper for free from nearby stationery stores, printing shops, wallpaper stores, or at their workplaces.

Once the materials are assembled, decide with your child on an easily accessible location for the Writer's Box.

Making Lists

Make lists with your child and let them see that one practical purpose of writing is to help us remember things. Just think of how often we make lists in our daily lives—lists of groceries to buy, chores to do, places to go, or people to call.

Keep a handy supply of note pads and notepaper available, so your child can easily help with your lists. Get your child to make his own lists: friends to call to invite for a sleepover, birthday gift wish list, chores to do, and so on.

Using a Message Board

A family message board can help your child see that writing reminder notes is useful, and that will give her a real reason to practice writing. Once you have the message board—a chalkboard, whiteboard, calendar, refrigerator board, or bulletin board—decide with your child where to put it. Be sure it's at an appropriate height for your child to use. Compose messages with your child, and leave them on the message board for other family members to read.

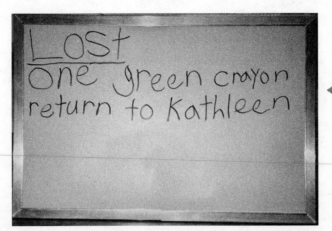

◀ *Kathleen left a message for her family.*

Creating Greeting Cards, Thank-You Notes, Post Cards, and Letters

Writing birthday cards, thank-you notes, post cards, and letters are just a few possible opportunities for you and your child to share in writing. Your child may want to use some of her Writer's Box materials to create original stationery or a software program such as Print Shop™ to design letters and cards on the computer. It's helpful to talk to children about what they'll draw or write before they begin so they can "rehearse" what they plan to put down on paper. Be sure to mail the letters or cards your child writes. Children delight in receiving a response to something they've written.

With the help of her mother—and the computer—Susan created an invitation to her birthday party.

Telecommunicating With a Computer

Helping your child telecommunicate through electronic mail or by surfing the Internet can be lots of fun—and provide lots of writing practice. A computer, a modem, a telecommunication software program, and a connection to a service provider are all you need. Surfing the World Wide Web to write letters to a favorite sports or television star or gathering information on a topic of interest or using e-mail to send a message to a family member are great ways for you and your child to share in writing.

Quick Tip

If many of your students have computers at home, invite parents to submit their e-mail addresses. Then parents and students can send messages to each other from home to school and school to home. You might also give your e-mail address to students and parents so you can send messages to your students and their parents, and they can respond.

E-Mail Message　　　　**September 28, 1997 - 7:30 p.m.**

TO:　Aunt Mary
FROM:　Candice

Hi Aunt Mary,

Can you come to my soccer game the weekend you come to Greene in October? We won two games and lost two games. My favorite position is Center Forward. We are learning cursive in school. It is lots of fun. I am in dance.

What are you doing in school? How are Jay and Sam?

Love,
Candice

Keeping a Travel Journal

A travelog will keep your child writing! Consider keeping a travel journal when the family goes on an extended vacation. Recording the special events and happenings on a family trip is an ideal way for you and your child to write together. Include drawings, photographs, and travel memorabilia in the journal. Later on, you'll delight in reliving the vacation by rereading the account and remembering what you saw, experienced, and enjoyed.

I went to Disney World.

◀ *Misha Flom kept a travel journal when he went to Disney World.*

Classroom Newsletters

Many Centre Ridge and Halley teachers regularly use newsletters to inform parents about what's going on in their classrooms. The newsletter is a good way to explain your writing program. In addition to your own explanations, you can involve your students by having them write about what they are learning about writing, or have them give tips for writing. You'll be indirectly letting parents know how to encourage their young writers. Plan to incorporate one idea about writing every few weeks. Here are a couple of samples of what our teachers and students have written in parent newsletters:

Teacher Sample

Creating a Home Writing Environment

In the classroom, I frequently model for your children how I write. As parents, you can also share with your child how you use writing in your daily life. Call attention to the writing you do for your job, model the resources you use for writing (dictionaries environmental print, spell check on the computer), and set an example by letting them see you write!

Student Sample

Quotation Marks
by Barbara Peck

We learned to use punctuation in our class this week. We learned about quotation marks. We looked in some of the big books we read and saw how real authors use quotation marks. Then, we used quotation marks in our shared writing story about The Three Little Pigs. When we have conversation in our writing, we will try to put quotation marks.

*I*n this chapter, we've discussed some ways to inform parents about how young writers develop and how to involve parents in encouraging and supporting their young writer at home. We've found that parents always respond when they believe they are contributing to their child's school success. We hope you'll try a few of our suggestions to encourage writing at home and that these will help you discover other ways for your particular students.

Look for resources in the following appendix to use for all the activities and suggestions we've mentioned throughout the book.

APPENDIX

Bibliography

Assessment Forms

Bibliography

Publisher Information

Creative Teaching Press
Abrams & Company Publishers, Inc.
61 Mattatuck Heights
Waterbury, CT 06705
1-800-227-9120

Emergent literacy books to support shared, guided, and independent reading; easy content area books

Curriculum Associates, Inc.
North Billerica, MA 01862
1-800-225-0248
Wordless familiar big book tales; blank books

Demco, Inc.
P. O. Box 7488
Madison, WI 53707-7488
1-800-356-1200

Binding-machine and plastic bindings; school supplies

DLM
One DLM Park
Allen, TX 75002
1-800-527-4747

Stick-on type notes for writing text on wordless books

Dominie Press
1949 Kellogg Avenue
Carlsbad, CA 92008
1-800-232-4570

Old and new familiar tales in big- and small-book versions; letter books

Edukits, Inc.
1089 Memorex Drive
Santa Clara, CA 95050
1-800-433-8548

Writing resources such as magnetic letters; magnetic chalkboards; whiteboards; white tape

Felt Educational Products
Storyteller, Inc.
19900 Stough Farm Road
Cornelius, NC 28031
1-888-470-FELT

Washable storyboards; hand puppets; felt fairy tales and nursery rhymes

Great Source Education Group
181 Ballardvale Street
Wilmington, MA 01887
1-800-289-4490

Language reference books for first and second grades

Markerboard People
2300 Spikes Lane
Lansing, MI 48906
1-800-828-3375

Whiteboards and chalkboards with accompanying markers

Newbridge Educational Publishing
P.O. Box 6002
Delran, NJ 08370-6002
1-800-867-0307

Emergent literacy big books and small-book versions; includes many content area subject titles

Perfection Learning
1000 North Second Avenue
P. O. Box 500
Logan, IA 51546-1099
1-800-831-4190

Hardcover and softcover blank books in a variety of sizes and shapes

Rand McNally
P.O. Box 1906
Skokie, IL 60076-8906
1-800-678-7263

Reference materials for primary students

Resources For Reading
P.O. Box 9
La Honda, CA 94020-0009
1-800-278-7323

Writing resources such as magnetic letters; magnetic chalk and white boards; white tape

Rigby
P.O Box 797
Crystal Lake, IL 60039-0797
1-800-822-8661

*Familiar tales, poems, and rhymes on charts or in big- and small-book versions;
letter books*

Scholastic, Inc.
2931 East McCarty Street
Jefferson City, MO 65101
1-800-724-6527

*Old and new favorite tales; nursery rhymes; reference materials; content area subject
titles in big- and small-book versions*

Treetop Publishing
P. O. Box 085567
Racine, WI 53408-5567
1-414-884-0501

Hardcover blank books in a variety of sizes

Wikki Stix Company
2432 W. Peoria Avenue, Suite 1188
Phoenix, AZ 85029
1-800-869-4554

Non-toxic, waxed yarn for highlighting text and forming letters

Wright Group
19201-120th Avenue, N. E.
Bothell, WA 98011
1-800-648-2970

*Old and new favorite tales, poems, and nursery rhymes in big- and small-book
versions; letter books*

Professional Resources

Areglado, Nancy, & Dill, Mary. (1997). *Let's Write.* New York: Scholastic.

Blevins, Wiley. (1998). *Phonics from A–Z.* New York: Scholastic.

Butler, Andrea, & Turbill, Jan. (1987). *Towards a Reading-Writing Classroom.* Portsmouth, NH: Heinemann.

Calkins, Lucy McCormick. (1994). *The Art of Teaching Writing.* Portsmouth, NH: Heinemann.

Clay, Marie. (1991). *Becoming Literate.* Portsmouth, NH: Heinemann.

———. (1993). *An Observation Survey.* Portsmouth, NH: Heinemann.

Cunningham, Patricia. (1995). *Phonics They Use: Words For Reading and Writing.* Reading, MA: Addison-Wesley.

Fountas, Irene C., & Pinnell, Gay Su. (1996). *Guided Reading: Good First Teaching For All Children.* Portsmouth, NH: Heinemann.

Graves, Donald. (1994). *A Fresh Look at Writing.* Portsmouth, NH: Heinemann.

Hall, Nigel, & Robinson, Anne. (1995). *Looking at Literacy.* London, England: David Fulton.

Heard, Georgia. (1995). *Writing Toward Home.* Portsmouth, NH: Heinemann.

Holdaway, Don. (1979). *The Foundations of Literacy.* Sydney, Australia: Ashton Scholastic.

Irvine, Joan. (1987). *How to Make Pop-Ups.* New York: William Morrow.

Johnson, Paul. (1991). *A Book of One's Own: Developing Literacy Through Making Books.* Portsmouth, NH: Heinemann.

———. (1993). *Literacy Through the Book Arts.* Portsmouth, NH: Heinemann.

Learning Media, Ministry of Education. (1992). *Dancing With the Pen.* Wellington, New Zealand: Ministry of Education. Katonah, NY: Richard C. Owen.

———. (1997). *Reading For Life: The Learner as a Reader.* Wellington, New Zealand: Ministry of Education. Katonah, NY: Richard C. Owen.

————. (1985). *Reading in Junior Classes*. Wellington, New Zealand: Ministry of Education. Katonah, NY: Richard C. Owen.

Leu, Jr., Donald, & Leu, Deborah Diadiun. (1997). *Teaching With the Internet: Lessons From the Classroom*. Norwood, MA: Christopher-Gordon.

Linse, Caroline T. (1997). *The Treasured Mailbox*. Portsmouth, NH: Heinemann.

Moline, Steve. (1995). *I See What You Mean: Children at Work with Visual Information*. York, ME: Stenhouse.

Mooney, Margaret. (1990). *Reading To, With, and By Children*. Katonah, NY: Richard C. Owen.

Opitz, Michael. (1996). *Getting the Most From Predictable Books*. New York: Scholastic.

Peterson, Ralph. (1992). *Life in a Crowded Place*. Portsmouth, NH: Heinemann.

Pugliano-Martin, Carol. (1998). *25 Just-Right Plays for Emergent Readers*. New York: Scholastic.

Richey, Virginia H., & Tuten-Puckett, Katharyn E. (1993). *Using Wordless Picture Books: Authors and Activities*. Englewood, CO: Teacher Ideas Press.

Smith, Frank. (1982). *Writing and the Writer*. Fort Worth, TX: Harcourt Brace College Pub.

Vgotsky, Lev. (1962). *Thought and Language*. Cambridge, MA: M. I. T. Press.

————. (1978). *Mind in Society: The Development of Higher Psychological Processes*. Cambridge, MA: Harvard University Press.

Zike, Dinah. (1989). *Big Book of Books and Activities*. San Antonio, TX: Dinah-Might Activities.

Children's Literature Selections

Nursery Rhymes

Butterworth, Nick. (1991). *Nick Butterworth's Book of Nursery Rhymes*. New York: Viking Penguin.

Children's Television Workshop & Rigby. (1998). *Jumbled Tumbled Tales & Rhymes*. Crystal Lake, IL: Reed Elsevier.

Chorao, Kay. (1994). *Mother Goose Magic*. New York: Dutton Books.

dePaola, Tomie. (1985). *Tomie dePaola's Mother Goose*. New York: Putnam.

Dyer, Jane. (1996). *Animal Crackers*. Boston: Little, Brown.

Hale, Sarah J. (1990). *Mary Had a Little Lamb*. New York: Scholastic.

James, Frances, (Ed.). (1996). *Cambridge Big Book of Nursery Rhymes*. New York: Dominie Press.

Lobel, Arnold, (Ed.). (1986). *Random House Book of Mother Goose*. New York: Random House.

Marzollo, Jean. (1986). *The Rebus Treasury*. New York: Dial Books.

Reid, Barbara. (1989). *Sing a Song of Mother Goose*. New York: Scholastic.

Slier, Debby (Ed.). (1995). *Real Mother Goose Book of American Rhymes*. New York: Scholastic.

Yolen, Jane, (Ed.). (1992). *Jane Yolen's Mother Goose Songbook*. Pennsylvania: Boyds Mill Press.

Poetry

Christelow, Eileen. (1989). *Five Little Monkeys Jumping on a Bed*. New York: Clarion Books.

de Regniers, Beatrice Schenk, Moore, Eva, White, Mary Michaels, & Carr, Jan (Eds.). (1988). *Sing a Song of Popcorn*. New York: Scholastic.

Hopkins, Lee Bennett (Ed.). (1988). *Side By Side Poems to Read Together*. New York: Simon & Schuster.

Prelutsky, Jack (Ed.). (1983). *Random House Book of Poetry for Children.* New York: Random House.

Rees, Mary. (1988). *Ten in a Bed.* New York: Little, Brown.

Rosen, Michael. (1989). *We're Going On a Bear Hunt.* Old Tappan, NJ: Simon & Schuster Children's.

Westcott, Nadine. (1988). *The Lady With The Alligator Purse.* Boston: Little, Brown.

Songs

Cauley, Lorinda Bryan. (1989). *Old MacDonald Had a Farm.* New York: Putnam.

Conover, Chris. (1976). *Six Little Ducks.* New York: HarperCollins Children's.

Galdone, Paul. (1986). *Over in the Meadow.* New York: Simon & Schuster.

Kovalski, Mary Ann. (1987). *Wheels on the Bus.* New York: Little, Brown.

Peek, Merle. (1981). *Roll Over.* New York: Houghton Mifflin.

Rae, Mary M. (1988). *Farmer in the Dell.* New York: Viking Kestrel.

Raffi. (1989). *Five Little Ducks.* New York: Crown.

Rigby. (1998). *KinderChants.* Crystal Lake, IL: Reed Elsevier.

Rounds, Glen. (1990). *I Know an Old Lady.* New York: Holiday House.

Scelsa, Greg. (1994). *Down on the Farm.* Cypress, CA: Creative Teaching Press.

Twinn, M. (1997). *Old Macdonald Had a Farm.* Singapore: Child's Play (International) Ltd.

Watten, Cynthia & Poe, Ken (Ed.). *Mary Wore Her Red Dress.* CA: Teaching Resource Center.

Westcott, Nadine B. (1980). *I Know an Old Lady.* Boston: Little, Brown.

Wordless Books

Carle, Eric. (1987). *Do You Want To Be My Friend?*. New York: Thomas Y. Crowell.

Day, Alexandra. (1991). *Carl's Afternoon in the Park*. New York: Farrar, Straus & Giroux.

———. (1985). *Good Dog, Carl*. New York: Scholastic.

DePaola, Tomie. (1978). *Pancakes For Breakfast*. Florida: Harcourt Brace Jovanovich.

Goodall, John. (1988). *Little Red Riding Hood*. Old Tappan, NJ: Simon & Schuster Children's.

Martinez, Estefanita. (1992). *The Naughty Little Rabbit and Old Man Coyote*. Chicago: Children's Press.

Mayer, Mercer. (1971). *A Boy, a Dog, a Frog, & a Friend*. New York: Dial Books.

———. (1976). *Hiccup*. New York: Dial Books.

McCully, Emily Arnold. (1985). *First Snow*. USA: Harper Trophy.

———. (1988). *New Baby*. USA: Harper Trophy.

Ormerod, Jan. (1982). *Moonlight*. New York: Lothrop, Lee & Shepard Books.

———. (1981). *Sunshine*. New York: Lothrop, Lee & Shepard Books.

Prater, John. (1985). *The Gift*. New York: Viking Penguin.

Rathmann, Peggy. (1994). *Good Night, Gorilla*. New York: G. P. Putnam's Sons.

Schories, Pat. (1991). *Mouse Around*. New York: Farrar.

Turkle, Brinton. (1976). *Deep in the Forest*. New York: E. P. Dutton.

Ward, Nick. (1987). *The Surprise Present*. New York: Oxford University Press.

Wildsmith, Brian. (1997). *The Apple Bird*. New York: Oxford University Press.

———. (1997). T*he Trunk*. New York: Oxford University Press.

Predictable Stories

Barton, Byron. (1995). *Buzz, Buzz, Buzz.* Old Tappan, NJ: Simon & Schuster Children's.

————. (1991). *The Three Bears.* USA: HarperCollins.

Becker, John. (1991). *Seven Little Rabbits.* New York: Scholastic.

Bender, Robert. (1993). *The Three Billy Goats Gruff.* New York: Henry Holt.

Capucilli, Alyssa Satin. (1995). *Inside a Barn in the Country.* New York: Scholastic.

Cowley, Joy. (1991). *Greedy Cat.* New York: Richard C. Owen Publishers.

Gag, Wanda. (1956). *Millions of Cats.* New York: Scholastic.

Green, Susan. (1992). *The Three Little Pigs.* San Diego, CA: Dominie Press.

Hutchins, Pat. (1968). *Rosie's Walk.* Old Tappan, NJ: Simon & Schuster Children's..

Kimmel, Eric. (1993). *The Gingerbread Man.* New York: Holiday House.

Lowell, Susan. (1992). *The Three Little Javelinas.* New York: Scholastic.

MacDonald, Margaret Read. (1995). *The Old Woman Who Lived in a Vinegar Bottle.* Little Rock, AK: August House LittleFolk.

McQueen, Lucinda. (1987). *Little Red Hen.* New York: Scholastic.

Numeroff, Laura Joffe. (1991). *If You Give a Moose a Muffin.* New York: HarperCollins.

————. (1985). *If You Give a Mouse a Cookie.* New York: HarperCollins.

————. (1998). *If You Give a Pig a Pancake.* New York: HarperCollins.

Parkes, Brenda. (1986). *Who's in the Shed?* Crystal Lake, IL: Rigby.

Smith, Judith, & Parkes, Brenda. (1993). *The Gingerbread Man.* Crystal Lake, IL: Rigby.

————. (1993). *The Little Red Hen.* Crystal Lake, IL: Rigby.

————. (1993). *The Three Billy Goats Gruff.* Crystal Lake, IL: Rigby.

Steig, William. (1969). *Sylvester and the Magic Pebble*. New York: Simon & Schuster.

Ward, Cindy. (1988). *Cookie's Week*. New York: Scholastic.

Williams, Sue. (1990). *I Went Walking*. San Diego, CA: Harcourt Brace & Company.

Wood, Audrey & Don. (1984). *The Napping House*. San Diego, CA: Harcourt, Brace, Jovanovich.

Informational Books

Berger, Melvin. (1993). *Squirrels All Year Long*. New York: Newbridge Communications.

Sill, Cathryn. (1991). *About Birds*. Atlanta, GA: Peachtree Publishers, LTD.

Children's Reference Materials

Curriculum Associates, Inc. (1995). *Spellex Thesaurus*. North Billerica, MA: Author.

(1993). *Discovery Atlas of the United States*. Skokie, IL: Rand McNally.

Editors of American Heritage Dictionary. (1998). *American Heritage Picture Dictionary*. New York: Houghton Mifflin.

Editors of Scholastic. (1996). *Scholastic Children's Dictionary*. New York: Scholastic.

Ganeri, Anita. (1992). *Picture Atlas of the World*. Auburn, ME: Ladybird Books.

Hobson, E. W., (Ed.). (1994). *A Basic Dictionary: A Student's Reference*. Baltimore, MD: Ottenheimer Publishers.

Hook, Sue, & Royston, Angela. (1995). *A First Atlas*. New York: Scholastic.

Kemper, Dave, Elsholz, Carol, & Sebranek, Patricia. (1997). *Write One*. Wilmington, MA: Great Source Educational.

Kemper, Dave, Nathan, Ruth, & Sebranek, Patrick. (1996). *Write on Track.* Wilmington, MA: D. C. Heath.

Kespert, Deborah, & Asser, Kate, (Eds.). (1996). *Picture Reference Atlas.* Chicago: World Book.

Levey, Judith S., (Ed.). (1990). *Macmillan First Dictionary.* Old Tappan, NJ: Simon & Schuster Children's.

————. (1991). *Picture Word Book.* New York: Macmillan.

Paton, John. (1992). *The Kingfisher Children's Encyclopedia.* New York: Kingfisher Books.

Pye, Wendy. (1994). *My First Dictionary.* Bothell, WA: Wright Group.

Reed, Langford. (1985). *The Writer's Rhyming Dictionary.* Boston: Writer, Incorporated.

Schiller, Andrew. (1978). *In Other Words, A Junior Thesaurus.* New York: Lothrop, Lee & Shepard Books.

Windridge, C. (1993). *Choose Your Words A School Thesaurus.* Baltimore, MD: Ottenheimer Publishers.

Young, Sue. (1994). *The Scholastic Rhyming Dictionary.* New York: Scholastic.

Computer Software Selections

Broderbund Software. (1993). Print Shop. Macintosh & Windows versions. San Rafael, CA: Broderbund.

Students can create their own greeting cards, letterheads, banners, and signs.

Claris Corporation. (1995). ClarisWorks 4.0. Macintosh version. Santa Clara, CA: Claris.

A word processing, database, spreadsheet, draw and paint program used to create books, newsletters, and slide shows.

Davidson & Associates, Inc. (1992). Kid Works 2. Macintosh and Windows versions. Torrance, CA: Davidson & Associates.

Students can write, illustrate, and listen to their own stories and print a small-book version.

Edmark Corporation. (1996). Kid Desk. Macintosh & Windows versions. Redmond, WA: Edmark.

Students can create e-mail and voice-mail messages to others sharing the same computer; interactive calendar, address card file, and note pad.

Edmark Corporation. (1994). Imagination Express Series. Macintosh & Windows versions. Redmond, WA: Edmark.

Students can create animated electric books in a marine sanctuary, medieval castle, rain forest, pyramids, colonial towns, or neighborhood.

Edmark Corporation. (1996). Stanley's Sticker Stories. Macintosh and Windows versions. Redmond, WA: Edmark Corporation.

Students can create their own stories and can print copies of their book.

The Learning Company. (1997). Paint, Write & Play! Macintosh & Windows versions. Minneapolis, MN: The Learning Company.

Students can paint pictures and create letters, stories, and poems with text-to-speech capabilities.

The Learning Company. (1994). Storybook Weaver Deluxe. Macintosh & Windows versions. Minneapolis, MN: The Learning Company.

Students can create and write stories.

The Learning Company. (1991). The Writing Center: School Edition. Macintosh version. Fremont, CA: The Learning Company.

Student-friendly word processing- and desktop-publishing software program.

Roger Wagner Publishing, Inc. (1993-98). HyperStudio. Macintosh & Window versions. El Cajon, CA: Roger Wagner Publishing.

Multimedia software that allows students to write, add animation and sound, and even incorporate the internet into their writing.

Alphabet Recognition Sheet

Name_____ Date_____

✔ = correct response, i.e. Alphabet Name, Letter Sound or Word
● = incorrect response

	letter	sound	word		letter	sound	word
A				a			
E				e			
X				x			
M				m			
Q				q			
U				u			
G				g			
B				b			
F				f			
J				j			
T				t			
R				r			
V				v			
N				n			
C				c			
Y				y			
K				k			
O				o			
I				i			
W				w			
D				d			
L				l			
S				s			
P				p			
Z				z			
H				h			
				a			
				g			

Total Correct: _____   Total Correct: _____

Comments:

Adapted from An Observation Survey by Marie Clay

Getting the Most Out of Morning Message and Other Shared Writing Lessons   Scholastic Professional Books

Student Alphabet Chart

A	E	X	M	Q	U	G
B	F	J	T	R	V	N
C	Y	K	O	I	W	D
L	S	P	Z	H		
a	e	x	m	q	u	g
b	f	j	t	r	v	n
c	y	k	o	i	w	d
l	s	p	z	h	a	g

Writing Sample Assessment Record For Early Writing

Name_____ Date(s)_____

To build a profile of the writer use a different colored highlighter pen to mark the learning behaviors observed each time a writing sample is reviewed. In the comments section make a note or two about future areas of focus.

Concepts/Conventions of Print

Knows where to begin writing
Knows writing moves left-to-right and top-to-bottom
Leaves spaces between words
Correct letter formation
Concept of letter
Concept of word
Uppercase and lowercase letters used conventionally
Approximate spelling
Conventional spelling of frequently used words
Uses punctuation: periods; question marks; exclamation marks; quotations; commas; apostrophes
Other: _____

_____

Understands That Writing Conveys a Message

Drawing/pictures
Scribble
Print-like symbols
Strings of letters
Writes own name: first name; last name
Letter/sound relationships: beginning; beginning/ending; beginning/medial/ending
Labels for pictures
Words
Phrases (groups of words)
Sentence
Several sentences
Beginning, middle and end
Details or vocabulary specific to topic
Central idea organized and elaborated
Other: _____

_____

Comments:

Getting the Most Out of Morning Message and Other Shared Writing Lessons   Scholastic Professional Books

Designed by Mary Browning Schulman and Carleen daCruz Payne